# SECRET
# BOLTON

## Ray Jefferson

AMBERLEY

# About the Author

Ray Jefferson is chairman of Bolton Documentary Photography, past president of the Bolton Camera Club, and an active Rotarian. Ray used to work for Bolton Borough Council and now spends much of his time volunteering in various capacities where he can bring his photography to bear on projects of benefit to the town. He is well known in the area.

First published 2021

Amberley Publishing
The Hill, Stroud
Gloucestershire, GL5 4EP

www.amberley-books.com

ISBN  978 1 4456 5486 7 (print)
ISBN  978 1 4456 5487 4 (ebook)

British Library Cataloguing in Publication Data.
A catalogue record for this book is available from the British Library.

Typesetting by SJmagic DESIGN SERVICES, India.
Printed in Great Britain.

# Contents

# Introduction

Who knew?

If that is the reader's reaction to some of the things found in this short book, then the writing will have been worthwhile. A lot has been written about the history of Bolton and its surrounding towns over the last 200 years, so what can be said that is entirely new? Well, not much of course, although some interesting gems can be found in the archives, as well as new sidelights on some otherwise well-known stories. These supply many of the ingredients for this book, together with topics which I feel contribute to the understanding of the town as we find it today.

The book does not attempt to give a balanced picture of the past. Rather, I have attempted to take the reader on a pleasant meander around topics which have interested, bemused, or surprised me. The contents owe a great debt to the authors of the many books and pamphlets which have been written over the years, as well as to the Bolton Library and Museums Service, the British Newspaper Archive and the wealth of information generally available on the internet. Where sources have been found to contradict each other, I have strived to determine the truth of the matter, but mistakes are inevitable. Blame me.

Many of the photographs have been taken by me, but where others are responsible, I have named the sources. Every attempt has been made to seek permission for copyright material used in this book. However, in this digital age, all too often the original photographer or copyright holder is unknown and, if I have inadvertently used such material without permission/acknowledgement, I apologise and will make the necessary correction at the first opportunity.

Ray Jefferson

# 1. Beginnings

## Glaciers

The bedrock under Bolton is complex with much faulting, but, in general, the town lies on coal measures overlain in places by new red sandstone. Beneath this lies millstone grit which outcrops to form the higher moorland to the north of Bolton around Winter Hill and Rivington Pike. Many of the details in the landscape show the effects of glaciation where boulder clays and gravels have been left behind over wide areas by retreating glaciers 9,000 or more years ago.

Today we have a good understanding about the behaviour of glaciers and ice-sheets and the various landforms they produce. During the second half of the nineteenth century however there was considerable controversy about the action of ice and just how it had affected the land. One of the exponents of the theory which is accepted today was a young American geologist called Henry Carvill Lewis.

When Henry graduated with the highest honours in the natural sciences from the University of Pennsylvania at the age of twenty-two, he had high hopes of making a significant impact in his chosen field of geology. True, he had other interests, including

A landform of hummocks created from glacial deposits near Horwich.

Glacial deposits seen in a stream bank at Gingham Brow, Horwich.

Henry Carvill Lewis.

astronomy, but geology was his calling. What he could not have known however was the major contribution he was destined to make to the understanding of the last ice age and his permanent relationship with Bolton, and the village of Walmsley in particular.

Henry initially took a conventional route at university by studying the classics, but soon moved on to the natural sciences for his master's degree. After graduation he volunteered to work for the Geological Survey of Pennsylvania where he was active for around five years. During that time, he helped trace the great terminal glacial moraines which cross the northern part of his home state. Moraines had long been understood to be the result of glaciers depositing rock debris as they made their way down from northern latitudes during the ice age. However, there was a continuing controversy about the precise mechanisms involved, some believing the debris had fallen from underneath glaciers floating on seas much higher than today, while others thought glaciers and ice sheets had progressed across dry land, grinding and ploughing up the bedrock to leave the evidence behind when the ice retreated as the climate warmed.

It was during this period that Henry was appointed as Professor of Mineralogy in the Academy of Natural Sciences, Philadelphia (1880) and Professor of Geology in Haverford College, Pennsylvania (1883). He also took the time to court and marry Julia Foulke in 1882. Her father had been the first person to discover a full dinosaur skeleton in North America and, perhaps unsurprisingly, she proved to be an important support for Henry in his subsequent research and travels.

Having published extensively on the glacial features of North America, Henry was eager to investigate whether, as he expected, similar features could be found in Europe.

As a consequence, he crossed the Atlantic with his wife and their baby daughter Gwendolen and, during the three summers of 1885 to 1887, he was the first to discover the terminal moraines left by the ice sheets advancing across Ireland, Wales and England during the last ice age, including those near to Manchester and York.

The couple travelled extensively by train and on foot with many of Henry's observations being made from a moving railway carriage window, no doubt with the notes being made by Julia. One of his train journeys took him from Manchester, through Bolton to Chorley and around. The notes from the journey say that

> hills covered in drift [glacial deposits] occur beyond Bolton; but not at Lostock Junction – these are seen to be made of rock, with no proof of glaciation. About Horwich Junction are low hills (of drift?), but no characteristic moraines. Rock outcrops at Adlington. About Chorley are a number of rounded drift hills ... On the south side of the tunnel above Entwistle is some drift containing many rounded boulders of local sandstone, &c.

Henry correctly identified the diverse spread of glacial deposits across the Bolton area which have subsequently been identified in detail by the British Geological Survey.

From his observations Henry argued that the landforms he observed were indeed the result of erosion and deposition by glaciers and ice sheets moving across the landscape, and not caused by debris falling from the undersides of melting icebergs floating across an extensive primaeval sea.

On 3 July 1888 Henry set sail for Europe with his wife Julia for the last time. He probably drank tainted water on, or just before the voyage since he subsequently died of typhoid fever in his lodgings at Roslyn Villa in Victoria Park, Manchester on 21 July 1888 at the early age of thirty-four. Just before he died, and knowing his fate, he gave all his unfinished manuscripts to Julia and asked her to complete and publish them, which she duly did in 1894 with the help of the Reverend Dr Crosskey of Birmingham.

Henry was buried in Walmsley church graveyard on 24 July 1888. The vicar of Walmsley, the Reverand John Stott, conducted the service which was attended by colleagues who had travelled with him from America as well as British dignitaries. The Bolton cotton spinner Joseph Pickering Lord was there and one of his daughters arranged a display of flowers on the ground near to the grave spelling out the motto 'He loved the truth'. Henry's tombstone also confirms his love of studying the world – 'Lord, what Love had I unto Thy law, all the day long was my study in it'. It is very fitting that the geological map of Britain shows his grave to be in the very glacial deposits which he had come to study and which he had so ably described and correctly theorised about.

Julia stayed on in Europe with her daughter Gwendolen and, thirty-six years later in 1924, she too was buried in the grave at Walmsley. After her mother's death Gwendolen returned to the sunnier climes of California where she died in Santa Barbara in 1973. Today Henry's theories of glacial action and the spread of ice sheets across the British Isles during recent geological times are wholly accepted. But how many people know of the eminent professor who rests in Walmsley having been snatched away at the peak of his powers?

Henry Carvill Lewis's grave at Walmsley Church.

A close-up of Henry Carvill Lewis's grave.

## DID YOU KNOW?

An ancient burial mound containing a doubled-up skeleton was found in the Haulgh in 1825 when a new road was being constructed between Bolton and Bury, and a similar mound containing a skeleton was also found in 1838 when the foundations for Walmsley church were being dug. In 1851 a further ancient burial site was discovered on the west bank of the River Croal around a mile south-west of the parish church and 100 yards east of Manchester Road containing a cremation. Such finds confirm that the area around Bolton was settled at least to some degree before the Romans arrived.

## Early Settlements

Perhaps the earliest evidence of settlement in Bolton is to be found in the fragments of a megalithic stone circle on Cheetham Close, just near the border with Blackburn with Darwen. Thought to date from the early Bronze Age (2100 to 1500 BC), the circle measured around 18 metres in diameter and some say was associated with Druidism. Described in detail by Thomas Greenhalgh of Sharples in 1871, the circle was very soon after damaged – one authority says it was by a picnic party and another suggests it was caused by a farmer taking a sledgehammer to the remains to deter visitors.

A remnant of the stone circle on Cheetham Close.

Later, in the first century AD, the Romans settled in Lancashire when Julius Agricola established camps where we find Manchester, Warrington, Lancaster and Wigan today. The Romans also built two roads across the area. The one from Cheshire to Carlisle passed through Walkden, Chequerbent, Wingates, and Blackrod, and the second found its way from Manchester to Yorkshire passing through Affetside to the north of Bolton on its way to Ribchester.

After the Romans had left, a Saxon prince known as the King of Deira conquered what is now Lancashire by the middle of the sixth century. Two hundred years later the Vikings (or Norsemen) were raiding and finally settled much of the country in their turn, establishing their Danelaw over the north and east of England, including modern Lancashire and Bolton.

The area around Bolton at this time would have been sparsely populated with small hamlets and clearings sustaining a small number of people engaged in hunting, fishing and modest cultivation. Some larger settlements existed but would hardly be considered villages by modern standards. Even so, after the arrival of the Normans in the eleventh century the growth of the north of England was promptly put in reverse. William the Conqueror essentially wiped the slate clean, not only confiscating all the land and giving it to his chosen men, making them aristocrats, but also laying waste the northern shires and their people during a scorched earth campaign.

As part of the new settlement William gave Roger de Poitou 188 manors in north-west England, comprising all the land between the Ribble and the Mersey, including Bolton. By the early twelfth century much of the land had been subdivided and was held by under-lords. For example, the Barony of Manchester was created with Albert Greslet recorded as the first Baron under the superior rule of Roger de Poitou. The Barony extended as far as Farnworth, Anglezarke, Westhoughton, Turton, Harwood, Halliwell, Horwich, Little Lever and Lostock. Albert's son Robert added more land and he created an extensive hunting ground centred on Horwich Moor. This stretched from Anglezarke and Sharples in the north to Westhoughton, Farnworth and Kearsley in the south and probably formed the basis of the Royal Forest which followed. The forest appears to have surrounded Bolton rather than included it, with the settlement having a status of something more than a hamlet.

## DID YOU KNOW?

The devastation in south-east Lancashire by William the Conqueror was so complete that the area did not justify even a mention in the Domesday Book.

## The Royal Forest of Horwich

The Royal Forest of Horwich had a boundary some 16 miles in circumference and was under the care of the Lords of Manchester, being perhaps their most important holding. It was subject to special legal and customary controls aimed at protecting deer, hawks

A medieval hunting scene. (Metropolitan Museum of Art, New York)

and wild boars. Consisting of both woodland and pasture, and incorporating moorland and valley, it was a regular hunting place for the local nobility and an important source of income for the king. A survey of 1282 revealed that three foresters were responsible for policing the forest at Horwich as well as collecting payments for cattle and swine feeding, quarrying, honey collecting, etc. The foresters probably had rights to collect windfall wood and to claim the skins of any deer killed in the forest. They paid £4 each year for their appointment (or bailiwick), which suggests there must have been significant benefit to be derived from occupying the position. They were also allocated forty-two oxgangs of land (an oxgang was around 15 acres) to sustain them in 'bread, drink and victuals', thirty-three of these being in Lostock, Rumworth, Heaton, Halliwell and Sharples.

Sustaining the forest was very much a community endeavour. On reaching twelve years of age, people living there were required to swear an oath:

You shall true liegeman be
Unto the King's Majestie;
You shall no hurt do
The beasts of the forest unto;
Nor anything unto
That doth belong thereto.
The offences of others you shall not conceal,

But to the utmost you shall them reveal
Unto the officers of the forest,
Or to them that may see the same redressed.
All these things you shall see done,
So help your God at's holy doom.

Anyone who allowed their cattle to stray into the forest without a licence would be subject to a fine of 6*d*, or on a third offence, have their animals forfeited.

As a place for hunting, great store was placed on encouraging hawks to nest. Once nest building had started each year the foresters called on villagers to assemble in Horwich and required them to go through the forest to discover the nest sites. Once found, the foresters themselves were obliged to remain in the forest day and night, guarding the birds and their eggs until the feast of St Barnaby (11 June), fed with food provided by the villagers. When the chicks were hatched the villagers were then tasked to collect the youngsters from their nests and to deliver them to the foresters for training in falconry. In default of this task, a villager could be taken and punished at the court in Manchester.

## DID YOU KNOW?

The fireclays found alongside the coal seams in Rivington and Smithills were worked for stoneware and earthenware, and the clay from a coal mine in Little Lever was fired into the terracotta which was used in the world's first terracotta church at St Stephen's, Lever Bridge in the 1840s.

St Stephen and All Martyrs Church, Radcliffe Road. The first terracotta church.

# 2. Science and Industry

It is well known that Bolton's prosperity stems mainly from the growth of the textile industry, and particularly cotton spinning. The needs of the textile industry also spawned bleaching and finishing, engineering, and all the other supporting functions and services that have combined to give the town its unique heritage. Thanks to several local inventions, spinning and weaving evolved from their beginnings as a domestic cottage industry, required to bolster or even supplant agricultural earnings, into the large-scale mill-based processes which stimulated Bolton's rapid urban and industrial expansion from the late eighteenth century onwards.

The cotton industry reached its zenith in the early twentieth century, but after the First World War countries that had once depended on British textile exports began to develop their own industries, often using machinery supplied from Bolton engineering companies. The cotton trade entered a period of long-term decline which ultimately resulted in the demise of cotton spinning in the town altogether.

The current volume does not seek to explore the complex and fascinating development of Bolton's industrial history, but instead concentrates on a few of the perhaps lesser-known byways of science and innovation.

## The Amateur Astronomer

Moses Holden was born in Bolton in 1777 at a time when the amateur enthusiast could still make a significant mark on scientific understanding. He spent most of his life spreading knowledge about astronomy and enthusing others about the topic. As a young child Moses lived with his father, Thomas, and his elder brother, John, in Packhorse Street, Bolton, although the family moved to the Preston area when Moses was around seven. By the age of ten he became enthralled by the sky at night and soon learned about the life of Jeremiah Horrocks who, in 1639, was the first person to predict the transit of Venus across the face of the Sun. Moses never lost his admiration for the Liverpudlian astronomer and was later instrumental in commemorating his life.

Moses became a devout Methodist by his late teens, travelling around the Fylde to give sermons as a lay preacher, a peripatetic habit which was to continue throughout much of his life. Although he initially followed in his father's footsteps as a weaver, Moses wanted to share his enthusiasm for astronomy by becoming a travelling lecturer. He found some of the money to support this by constructing and selling telescopes and microscopes, laboriously grinding the lenses himself. He also constructed his own magic lantern and an orrery – an accurate working mechanical model to demonstrate the movements and the workings of the solar system – to illustrate his talks.

Sell-out crowds attended his lectures on the motion of celestial bodies at the Theatre Royal in Preston and between 1815 and 1828 he set out with his wife Isabella to take his

A SMALL

# Celestial Atlas,

OR

## MAPS OF THE VISIBLE HEAVENS,

IN THE LATITUDES OF BRITAIN;

DESIGNED AS A USEFUL COMPANION FOR

# THE YOUNG STUDENT,

AS WELL AS FOR THE

### PRACTICAL ASTRONOMER, ETC.

### By M. HOLDEN,

ASTRONOMER.

**THIRD EDITION, CORRECTED AND IMPROVED.**

Ὁι ὑρανοι διηγυνται δοξαν Θευ. Psalm xix. 1.

### MANCHESTER:

PRINTED FOR THE AUTHOR,

BY HARRISON AND CROSFIELD, MARKET STREET.

1834.

The cover of the *Celestial Atlas* by Moses Holden.

lectures to many towns across England. Indeed, two of his children were born away from home – William in Pontefract and John in Banbury. During this period, he also found time to publish an inexpensive *Celestial Atlas* which passed through several editions and which he no doubt sold alongside his lectures.

Towards the conclusion of his tours Moses was able to pay for a marble monument to Jeremiah Horrocks in Toxteth Park, where he was born, showing the planet Venus on the Sun's disc and inscribed with the words *Venus in Sole visa, November 24, 1639*. Moses also became a founder member of the Institute for the Diffusion of Knowledge which went on to become the Mechanics' Institute, the Preston Polytechnic and eventually led to the University of Central Lancashire.

In 1834 Moses was made a freeman of Preston and he remained active in his chosen discipline to a good age. He was still lecturing to appreciative audiences in 1844 when he was in such demand in Liverpool that he had to give three sets of lectures to satisfy

The Moses Holden telescope at the University of Central Lancashire. (UCLAN)

the public. He also continued his observations, measuring the transit of Mercury in 1848, estimating the size of sunspots in 1851 and commenting on the orbits of meteors at a British Association meeting in Liverpool in 1854. He died in 1864, at the age of eighty-seven.

In 2015 the Jeremiah Horrocks Institute for mathematics, physics and astronomy at Alston, north-east of Preston, became the proud owner of a 70-cm robotic telescope used for undergraduate teaching and the encouragement of public engagement in science. Very appropriately, this has been christened as the Moses Holden Telescope.

### DID YOU KNOW?

Joshua Routledge was a Yorkshire engineer who had moved to Bolton by 1811 and here his sister married the engineer Benjamin Hick. Joshua worked with the Bolton steam engine makers Thompson Swift & Co. and later had a hardware business at No. 26 Deansgate. In 1813 he patented an engineer's slide rule based on logarithmic scales, and published instructions for its use. He also made improvements to rotary steam engines, invented a portable machine to break stones for road repairs and helped extend the Wallsuches bleach works in Horwich. His slide rule became the basis for many other versions over the next century.

## The Bleachers and the Balloonist

Bleaching traditionally relied upon the time-consuming process of exposing cloth to sunlight on open crofts, but by the 1780s the use of chemical processes held out the prospect of an altogether faster and therefore profitable process. Two French chemists, Mathieu Vallet and Antoine Bourboulon de Boneuil, pioneered the development of chemical bleaching in England using chlorine.

Mathieu was born near Macon, south-west of Paris, in 1734, one of sixteen children whose father was a bleacher and master dyer. He learned the chemical side of his father's business and became a chemist, joining a factory at Javel, outside Paris, as an Associate Director in 1777. The main products made there were sulphuric and hydrochloric acids, important in many industrial processes.

Around this time, the Montgolfier brothers constructed a hot-air balloon which was first demonstrated in public near Lyon in 1783. On hearing of this, Antoine Bourboulon, who was also involved with the factory at Javel, suggested the use of hydrogen as a lifting medium. This required sulphuric acid to make the hydrogen, and there was, of course, one obvious supplier. In December 1783 Mathieu Vallet was tasked with filling a hydrogen balloon for its first flight, and the production of hydrogen for other flights followed. Buoyed by this success Mathieu and his partner Leonard Alban designed their own 10-metre-diameter balloon capable of carrying four passengers. They proceeded to make many flights near Paris in 1785–86, even being received by King Louis XVI and Marie Antoinette on one of their landings.

Meanwhile, in 1785 the French chemist Claude Louis Berthollet suggested the use of chlorine to bleach cloth and demonstrated his method at the Javel works, using hydrochloric acid to produce the chlorine gas which was absorbed into water for the bleaching process. Vallet and Alban saw the potential and refined the process in 1787 to make it an economic proposition.

Mathieu decided to leave France soon after to find his future in England. Perhaps he foresaw the French revolution. In any event, following a bankruptcy in France, Antoine Bourboulon de Boneuil soon joined him and they founded a company in Liverpool to manufacture bleaching fluid. Clearly, they had their sights on the rapidly expanding cotton industry of Lancashire as a prime market for their process. However, the outline of their method and its economic potential were already known among English bleachers and there was concern that Vallet and Bourboulon might achieve a patent and monopoly. To counter this the Society of Bleachers, based in Bolton, called a public meeting in Manchester in February 1788 to oppose any monopoly and to lobby for a patent which would exclude Vallet and Bourboulon. The Bolton bleachers Peter Ainsworth and his son Richard joined the committee set up to make the case to parliament but their pleas were rejected. The process consequently became open for anyone to exploit.

Despite their disagreements, the Ainsworths employed Mathieu and his son Victor at their Halliwell bleachworks after 1789 in order to introduce their chemical process. The Vallets also erected bleaching apparatus for the Rothwell company, and probably others in Bolton. Evidence of their assimilation into local society is found in Victor's admission to the Bolton Anchor and Hope Lodge of the Masons in February 1790 where the bleacher

Le Comte d'Artois Aerostat de Javel.

Cet Aerostat a été construit par M.M. Alban et Vallet pour constater la direction de ces Machines, d'après les essais annoncés dans les Journaux de X.^{bre} 1783. Janvier et Fev.^r 1784.

| | |
|---|---|
| A Soupape. | E Cercle de réunion |
| B Echelle de corde. | F Gondole. |
| C Equateur. | G Ailes. |
| D Tropique. | H Moulinet. |

Gravé par le Vachez M.^d d'Estampes aux Colonnade du Palais Royal.

Alban and Vallet's hydrogen balloon. (J. T. Towson)

# Anchor & Hope Lodge, No. 37, Bolton.

# ROLL OF MEMBERS

### FROM 1765.

Those marked * are Joining Members.

| Initiated or Joined. | Name. | When Installed W.M. | Remarks. |
|---|---|---|---|
| Aug. 10 | Richard Thornley | | Alehouse Keeper. |
| Oct. 12 | James Whalley | | Warehouseman. |
| Nov. 16 | William Bibby | | Comedian. |
| | Thos. Rothwell | | |
| 1787, Jan. 6 | John Makin | 27 Dec., 1792 | Innkeeper, Bolton. |
| Feb. 9 | John Mosley | | Innkeeper. |
| Aug. 2 | John Makinson | 27 June, 1792 | Cotton Manufacturer, Bolton. |
| 1788, Oct. 16 | George Mountain | | Innkeeper, Bolton. |
| Nov. 20 | Saml. Templeton Clarke | | Comedian, Bolton. |
| 1789, Mar. 12 | John Williams | { 24 June, 1790 27 Dec., 1798 } | Surgeon, Bolton. |
| 1790, Feb. 6 | Victor Vallett | | Chemist, Bolton. |
| Mar. 4 | Francis Wood | | Hatter. |
| 1791, Mar. 24 | Thomas Thornley | | Dyer, Bolton. |

Victor Vallett joins the Anchor and Hope Masonic Lodge, 1790. (Bolton Freemasons)

Thomas Ridgeway had been installed in 1765 and Peter Ainsworth acted as treasurer from 1786 to 1806. Bourboulon meanwhile returned to France.

Around 1797 Peter and Richard Ainsworth and Victor Vallet joined forces to form a dyeing company which operated from a building known as 'chemical hall' in what is today appropriately called Valletts Lane in Halliwell. Unfortunately, the partnership was dissolved in March 1800 and Victor's bankruptcy followed seven months later. He probably disappeared back to France. The failure did not impact greatly on the Ainsworths

Valletts Lane and the former 'chemical hall' today.

however since they went on to buy the Smithills estate soon after and 'chemical hall' was converted into a line of weavers' cottages. Mathieu continued in England and was eventually buried in Childwall, outside Liverpool in 1823. The balloonist had finally come down to earth.

## DID YOU KNOW?

James Gregson, a blacksmith of Bolton, emigrated to the United States in 1837 where he and his wife Eliza soon set out on the Oregon trail to the west. They lived in Sutter's Fort, Sacramento until 1847. James was employed as a blacksmith by John Sutter and John Marshall to help construct a sawmill in Coloma in the Sierra Nevada foothills. While there Marshall discovered gold in the tailrace of the mill and he and Gregson went prospecting together. This ushered in the California gold rush of 1849.

## Further and Fatal Ballooning

Windham Sadler followed in his father James's footsteps in taking an interest in ballooning. His father made only the second ascent in the country from Manchester in 1785 and enjoyed several successful flights in the years that followed. Windham flew solo from Salford to Monk's Heath, near Knutsford in April 1824, as well as from Rochdale to Bacup, and Liverpool to Chester the following month. Thirty successful flights took place that summer, taking off from places such as Chester, Wigan and Drogheda in Ireland.

Finally, on 27 September 1824 Sadler ascended from the gasworks in Bolton, and a strong wind took him and his assistant, James Donnelly, north-eastwards. They decided to land at Fox Hill Bank, near Church, but had a major difficulty. The wind dragged the balloon along and broke their grappling iron. The basket eventually demolished a cottage chimney. At some point Sadler was thrown out of the basket but was caught by his feet in netting. He found himself suspended head downwards. He eventually fell to the ground and was found with a severe head injury, probably from striking the chimney. He died from his injuries the next day. Meanwhile the desperate James Donnelly travelled on, dislocating an arm when he was flung out at Cock Bridge, near Whalley. The balloon continued by itself and fell into the sea off the Yorkshire coast. Tragically, Mr Blenkinsop, the landlord of the Greyhound Inn to which Windham Sadler had been taken injured, also dropped dead from the shock of it all.

Ballooning continued as a public display however, and two years after Windham Sadler's demise Charles Green came to Bolton, also to fly from a site adjacent to the gasworks on Moor Lane. He was accompanied by the daughter of the gasworks manager, a Miss Spooner, who probably became the first Bolton person to make a flight.

## DID YOU KNOW?

In 1894 Bolton Corporation was given a telescope by Councillor T W Holden (possibly a relative of Moses Holden). The telescope was initially set up as part of the Chadwick Museum and used by the astronomy group of the Bolton Field Naturalists before the First World War. Having fallen into disrepair after the war, the telescope was donated to Bolton museum, where it is still possible to see parts of it today.

## Paper Making in Bolton

From the mid-seventeenth century the soft water running off the western Pennines helped the development of the paper industry, from Clitheroe in the north to Bolton in the south. The paper mills established in the Bolton and Farnworth areas were clustered around the rivers Croal and Irwell in particular. Creams paper mill on the River Irwell at Little Lever was established by James Crompton in 1677. James's younger brother Robert operated at Darley Hall, Farnworth from around 1690 until he died in 1737, and was followed by his son Ellis who built another mill on land owned by the Duke of Bridgewater at nearby Farnworth Bridge. Other mills were established at Springfield in 1820 (now the Trinity retail park) and by Ralph Crompton at Stoneclough.

In 1807 Henry and Sealy Fourdrinier patented a water-powered machine which allowed paper to be produced in a continuous roll rather than the single sheets previously made, although cutting into sheets by hand and careful drying was still needed. Thomas Bonsor Crompton, the great-grandson of Ellis Crompton, was running the mill at Farnworth Bridge by 1814, and he was convinced that he could improve the Fourdrinier machine by feeding the wet paper through a series of steam-heated cylinders. This greatly reduced the cost of production and was a fundamental breakthrough in the manufacture of paper. He secured a patent for his process in 1820, when he was only twenty-eight years old, and became wealthy by selling the machines to other paper makers even though the protection of his patent was soon lost because of a technicality. In 1828 he cooperated with Enoch Taylor to invent a rotary cutter to produce individual sheets more efficiently and its success was such that it was said that the Farnworth mill produced 2 per cent of all the nation's paper at one stage.

By 1842 the Farnworth Bridge works were being compared unfavourably with the Creams paper mill, perhaps because by then Thomas had developed other interests. He became the proprietor of the *Morning Post* as well as other newspapers. He was also a large cotton manufacturer at Prestolee employing up to 800 people in his mill there. He was a significant benefactor of Farnworth but also owned extensive moors in the Highlands.

St John's Church, Farnworth.

He died in 1858 at the home of his friend Thomas de la Rue in Bedfordshire and was buried in St John's Church, Farnworth where the great east end window is dedicated to his memory.

After Thomas Bonsor Crompton died the Farnworth paper mill passed to his nephew William J. Rideout who ran it until the business closed in 1883, brought on by an economic recession. The buildings stood empty until they eventually became the site of Champion's Bleachworks in 1894 which lasted until the buildings were demolished in the 1970s. The reservoirs for the mill remain today as a major feature in the Moses Gate country park.

Moses Gate Country Park.

# 3. The Growth of Local Government

## A Difficult Birth – Bolton Becomes a Borough

By the end of the eighteenth century the expansion of Bolton required a new way to pay for the public services needed. Considerable strain was being placed on the old methods of administration – the township, the parish vestry, and the Court Leet – relying on officers such as the boroughreeve, constables, moor lookers and scavengers to carry out the work to secure the well-being of the district. Such officers were often unpaid, and all ratepayers were expected to take their turn in office, threatening both competence and continuity. The town was also divided into two townships – Little Bolton to the north of the River Croal and Great Bolton to the south.

In 1792 it was agreed that the new way involved the enclosure of land. The Bolton Enclosure and Improvement Act was proposed and passed. Around 270 acres of Bolton

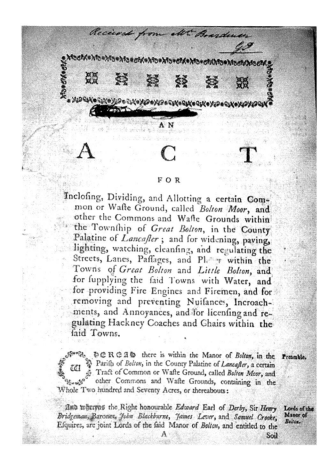

The first page of the 1792
Enclosure and Improvement Act.

Moor, to the south-west of the townships, was identified in the Act as common or waste land of little benefit to its owners. It was proposed to add this to the town, enclose the land, and to lay it out with roads and building plots to encourage well-ordered development. This would then generate an income from rents to pay for public services. Roads in the two townships themselves would be widened, paved, lit, watched and cleaned. Water was to be supplied, fire engines and firemen provided, and nuisances and annoyances prevented.

This bold step to expand the town could only succeed of course if there was indeed a demand for new building. That eventually proved to be the case since Bolton was in the throes of significant industrial and population growth. However, it was some time before this early form of town planning was carried through to completion, and some parts of the road layout for example were never achieved. Nevertheless, much of the area had been developed by 1850 and the main pattern of the roads laid out can still be traced today.

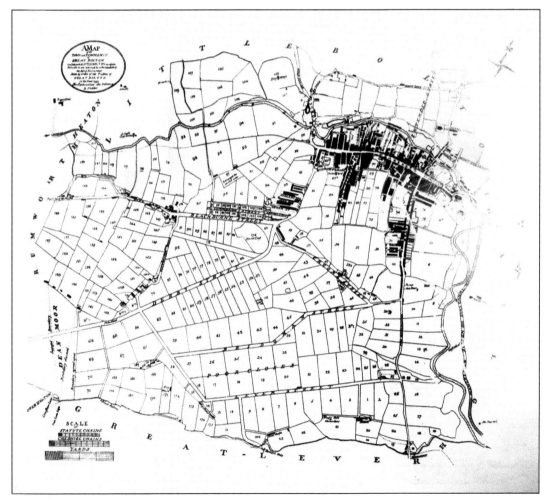

Map showing the town and extent of the Bolton Moor enclosures in 1792. (From the Collection of Bolton Library and Museum Services)

When the enclosure was completed, the estate was vested in two sets of trustees – one for Great Bolton and one for Little Bolton. Each trustee had to be resident in their town and possess a personal estate valued at £1,000 (in Great Bolton) or £500 (in Little Bolton) – considerable wealth. Politically, the trustees tended to be Tories, unlike the townships' former representatives who were more likely to be Liberal or Radical. The trustees, who met in private, were appointed for life and had the power to appoint their own replacements. They instigated a programme of highway improvement and construction which complemented the recent opening of the Manchester Bolton and Bury Canal. As well as other works, the Little Bolton trustees built themselves a town hall, and the Great Bolton trustees constructed a workhouse and laid out three public squares.

Meanwhile the older forms of government continued in parallel since the 1792 Act expressly safeguarded the rights and interests of the Lords of the Manor. In addition, there was no concerted management of the two townships together, so that, for example, a person causing an offence in one township could often find sanctuary in the other.

Some felt that the trustees could not in fact be trusted, being too inclined to use their position to promote their own interests. Consequently, a petition was raised to seek a charter for an elected local authority under the Municipal Corporations Act of 1835. The move was led by a Quaker, Henry Ashworth of Turton (the owner of Eagley Mills), and C. J. Darbyshire, a leading Liberal who subsequently became the town's first mayor. This step was taken in the teeth of opposition mounted by a Conservative/Anglican faction,

Little Bolton Town Hall.

Silverwell House, where a municipal charter for Bolton was first discussed.

supported by the Lords of the Manor, the trustees themselves and the town's Conservative MP, William Bolling. Nevertheless, in October 1838 Bolton became only the second town in England to achieve a Municipal Charter of Incorporation. It was a significant victory for the Liberals and Nonconformists, although the Act did not abolish the previous authorities and matters of local government consequently became very complicated. A vituperative political and legal dispute resulted, particularly about the cost of the new arrangements. The Conservatives refused to stand in municipal elections, declaring the charter to be illegal. Many people refused to pay their rates. The strength of feeling was illustrated when the *Bolton Chronicle* featured an article on 1 December 1838 about the first meeting of the council claiming that

> Such a medley of grotesque functionaries was never elected to serve a borough ... Notwithstanding a distinct section of the Act disqualifying all persons from serving as councillors who are suspected of 'lunacy', or 'imbecility of mind', certain persons have been appointed to consult upon Town matters, who have seldom been suspected of anything else.

The boroughreeves and constables of Great and Little Bolton actually published a formal notice in 1839 warning the public that the new charter was invalid, and that no person appointed by the Corporation had any authority to act as a constable. This was unhelpful at a time when the town was suffering a great deal of distress caused by unemployment and high food prices. Disturbances were imminent in support of the Chartist movement, arguing for universal suffrage, and troops had to be called out in August 1839 to quell riots at the parish church as well as Little Bolton town hall. In the end the administrative dispute was settled by the Boroughs Incorporation Act of 1842, which cemented the validity of the charter and tackled some of the overlap of powers.

The Conservatives accepted the situation and began to contest council seats, winning control of the council from the Liberals in 1844. The elections that year involved a bizarre element in that many people were accused of impersonation when casting votes. They were acquitted at trial when the defending counsel argued that the prosecution had not established the validity of the borough council to hold elections in the first place.

The trustees did not wish to give up their responsibilities easily and retained the income from Bolton Moor, the control of streets, sewers and markets as well as running their own parallel police force. The Board of Guardians continued to deal with poor relief and the vestries looked after burial grounds. To compound the problems of running the borough in a coherent way, there was continued distress in the town at this time because of a food shortage exacerbated by the Irish potato famine. Typhus fever and cholera outbreaks occurred in 1847 and 1848. In 1849 the Corporation's Sanitary Committee was already tackling offensive gutters, accumulations of noisome filth and cesspools, but because of the death toll from cholera and dysentery the Mayor, Thomas Rushton, took the initiative to urge the trustees of both Great and Little Bolton to transfer their powers

The plaque on Little Bolton Town Hall commemorating the 1839 riot.

to the Corporation so that a unified approach to the problem could be pursued. The trustees of Great Bolton agreed, subject to an Act of Parliament, but Little Bolton declined. In the event, and despite strong opposition, the Corporation obtained what they needed in the Bolton Improvement Act of 1850.

The Act was a major landmark. It made the Corporation the Local Board of Health and gave it the ability to tackle the sanitation problems. At last, both sets of trustees were disbanded, giving the Corporation full powers over the borough. Those unified powers also brought more uniform politics. The council was energised and major improvements in the town were soon underway.

## DID YOU KNOW?

In the mid-nineteenth century the Mayor of Bolton, Councillor Thomas Rushton, led the establishment of new and improved arrangements for the town. Accordingly, Thomas Bridson, R. S. Barlow and Stephen Blair MP presented Councillor Rushton with a Mayoral Chain and Seal in 1850. This is the same Mayoral Chain we have today. It originally had thirty-six gold links as well as a silver gilt seal, but over the years new links have been added by individual mayors so that the chain now consists of seventy-two links and a pendant badge. All the mayors between 1838 and 1941 are recognised by their individual links.

## The Struggle for Water

Good administration is one thing, but a copious supply of clean water in the home is another good measure of civilisation. Today everyone in Bolton can obtain that water by turning on their tap. What is sometimes not appreciated however is the immense effort over the years which has been required to create that supply.

As we have seen, in the early nineteenth century Bolton was a combination of two small, but fast-growing administrative areas (Great and Little Bolton). People relied on springs and wells for both industrial and domestic purposes and usually went to their nearest supply for water (sometimes even stealing from their neighbours). Sewage was handled in an insanitary manner and the serious contamination of water supplies became common as the population expanded.

The Enclosure Act of 1792 had specified that some of the income from the enclosure of Bolton Moor should be used to ensure that Great and Little Bolton were 'sufficiently supplied with good and wholesome water'. The Act allowed the construction of reservoirs on the moor for the supply of water to Great Bolton in particular. As things turned out, because of financial and political difficulties, the reservoirs on the moor were not constructed until fifty years later and meanwhile things continued in an unsatisfactory manner.

Given all the other priorities for action to improve the town the trustees felt unable to move fast on the water supply front. However, this changed in 1824 when the Great

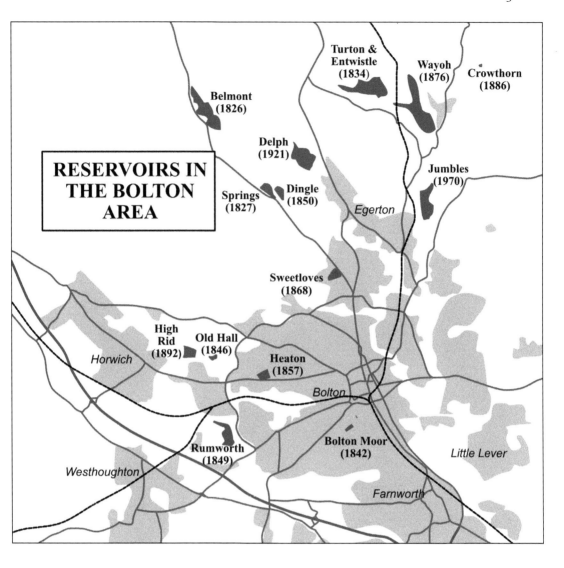

**RESERVOIRS IN THE BOLTON AREA**

Turton & Entwistle (1834)
Wayoh (1876)
Crowthorn (1886)
Belmont (1826)
Delph (1921)
Jumbles (1970)
Springs (1827)
Dingle (1850)
Egerton
Sweetloves (1868)
High Rid (1892)
Old Hall (1846)
Horwich
Heaton (1857)
Bolton
Rumworth (1849)
Bolton Moor (1842)
Little Lever
Westhoughton
Farnworth

and Little Bolton Waterworks Co. was established with the power to charge for supplies. This move had angered local radicals however who pointed out that many of the Great Bolton trustees were also shareholders in the new company and stood to profit from the situation at the expense of the poor.

The new company piped water to the town from the Dady Meadows spring above Sharples. This was soon followed by plans to construct the Springs reservoir, although before drinking water could be taken, a supply of 'compensation water' had to be provided for the industries which had previously relied on the same source. This required the construction of a second dam and reservoir (Belmont, 1826) purely for that purpose, the cost of which fell on the Waterworks Company (and therefore the consumers). The amount of water to be guaranteed in compensation was around 3.5 times the amount needed for the town's public supply and was exceptional for the time.

The panel announcing the Bolton Water Works on Belmont Road near the Springs reservoir.

Belmont reservoir.

Meanwhile, industrial demand, especially from bleachers, was growing and so in 1832 the construction of the Turton and Entwistle reservoir was authorised to control the supply of water from Bradshaw Brook. This quickly proved insufficient, and six years later the dam's embankment was raised to a level 125 feet above the bed of the brook. The works were completed by 1840 and the embankment was the highest in England until the Upper Barden reservoir was completed for Bradford.

By 1842 Bolton's population had risen to around 50,000 and it was proving difficult to keep up with the demand for water. That year, following pressure from the poor-law administrators, two reservoirs were at last built on Bolton Moor by the Waterworks Company to supply Great Bolton. This was a time of hardship in Lancashire and the construction was aided by a grant from the Manufacturing Districts Relief Fund. The project both gave work to unemployed operatives and supplied thirty-seven fountains for the 'poor of the borough', gratuitously and for ever. The reservoirs on the moor were not completely successful however since the water was tainted because of the highly manured land in their catchment area. The two reservoirs were finally closed in 1882.

Demand continued to grow inexorably. In 1843 the retitled Bolton Waterworks Company was empowered to build the Dingle reservoir. The millowners were flexing their muscles again and the water company was required to raise the level of the Belmont reservoir by 16 feet to give yet more compensation water. Proposals for Old Hall and Heaton reservoirs followed in 1846, although the Rumworth reservoir had also to be constructed to supply yet more compensation water. Pressure grew to bring the private

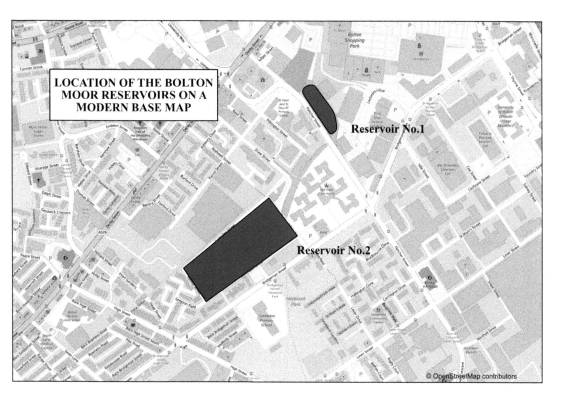

LOCATION OF THE BOLTON MOOR RESERVOIRS ON A MODERN BASE MAP

Reservoir No.1

Reservoir No.2

© OpenStreetMap contributors

Looking across the site of the original reservoirs on Bolton Moor today.

drinking water supplies under the control of the Conservative-led Corporation, even though the Liberals in opposition suspected that the acquisition price was inflated for the benefit of Conservative shareholders. Nevertheless, the council took ownership of the water company on 29 September 1847.

The works planned before the acquisition went ahead at a pace. The Rumworth reservoir was completed and the Belmont water level raised in 1849. The Dingle reservoir was opened in 1850. Heaton reservoir opened as late as 1857 however because of concerns about the likely quality of its water given the expansion of the urban area in that direction.

The drought of 1852 strained supplies and the council decided to try to obtain further water from the Belmont area. A bill was presented to parliament in April 1854, but it stirred up considerable opposition from millowners. They claimed that the flood waters which would be stemmed were important to them because they acted to cleanse the rivers which gave them their supplies (a little ironic since their activities were responsible for most of the pollution). The House of Lords rejected the bill and the council had to resort to more local supplies and commence the construction of the Heaton reservoir despite worries about water quality.

The supply of water became critical at the end of May 1854 with reserves for only fourteen days being available. The council did not wish to cut off manufacturers, but a meeting of millowners was called which agreed to the temporary abstraction of water from Middlebrook for domestic purposes. The continuing crisis meant that brewers were cut off at the end of June and this continued until at least August – a crisis indeed.

By 1863 the domestic supply from the Corporation waterworks was nearing its limit again even in good years and work commenced on the Sweetloves reservoir. Meanwhile another bill was presented to parliament to acquire the private Turton and Entwistle reservoir for

Rumworth reservoir.

Dingle reservoir.

the public water supply. This succeeded in 1865, but once again, strong opposition meant the Corporation had to construct the Wayoh reservoir to provide generous compensation supplies. As a consequence the domestic supply was slow in coming since the Turton and Entwistle reservoir could not be accessed until the completion of the Wayoh reservoir in 1876. The legislation also required over a quarter of the compensation water to be 'clear' – although that provision was probably unintended and was certainly a big mistake since industrial processes had previously not had water of such quality. The water from Wayoh had to be filtered at considerable cost – the only instance in the country, certainly up to 1947.

Beginning in 1878, Manchester proposed to take water from Thirlmere in the Lake District. In an unregulated world the scramble by large towns and cities to acquire control over major water catchments was in full swing. Approved in 1879 after a controversial passage through parliament, the Act allowed authorities in the vicinity of the aqueduct (including Bolton) to receive a share of the water. Construction was delayed until 1886 however, with the first water being taken in 1894.

The small Crowthorne reservoir needed to supply Edgworth and Entwistle was completed in 1886 and High Rid reservoir above Lostock followed in 1892. By 1901 the council was concerned again about securing supplies for the longer term. This led to proposals to use the Hodder Valley in Bowland, although these were abandoned as too expensive and other, more local solutions were sought. In 1905 five local reservoirs were authorised at Delph, Eagley, Hordern, Cadshaw and Broadhead. The Delph reservoir commenced construction in 1908. It was delayed by foundation problems and the outbreak of the First World War, but it was eventually brought into service in July 1921, supplying both drinking water and compensation water.

The proposed Eagley reservoir was proving an expensive proposition and it was realised that pollution from agriculture in its catchment would lead to high purification costs. Consequently, by 1916 it was agreed that the 1905 proposals should not be progressed beyond the Delph scheme and eyes were once again raised to distant valleys. By this time, the Hodder Valley was no longer available, having been taken to supply the Fylde. Other areas on the western slopes of the Pennines had also been taken to supply Lancaster, Preston and Blackburn. The further watersheds of the Lune valley were therefore considered.

The Corporation proposed to acquire and dam the watersheds tributary to the rivers Hindburn and Roeburn. There was considerable objection to Bolton's parliamentary bill from other authorities, local landowners, and from landowners in Bolton who would lose out because of the abandonment of the 1905 projects. The authorities adjacent to Bolton also objected since they felt that supplies should be planned by towns acting together rather than individually – much the same argument that was made later by Bolton itself against Manchester's Haweswater scheme. The Bolton bill was turned down. The Corporation was left with either their 1905 proposals, which appeared to be both expensive and risky, or the hope to join with Manchester on a possible Haweswater scheme.

Soon after, in 1919 Manchester did indeed firm up its plans to take water from Haweswater. Lancashire County Council challenged the proposal on the grounds that access to the water should be dealt with on a national basis. Bolton joined in as an objector. The objections succeeded in that Manchester was required to supply water at cost to the areas through which their aqueduct passed. Bolton had sought a preferential share of the water and the right to carry forward any unused supplies from year to year, but, unsurprisingly perhaps, Manchester could not agree to that.

Between the wars, slower population growth and the decline of the textile industry meant that the need for water did not expand as quickly as had been predicted in 1915. It was thought possible to survive until the Haweswater project came on stream. The foundation stone for the Haweswater dam was laid in April 1935. This had been a slow start, with works delayed since 1929 because of the recession. The first phase included a syphon across the Sprint valley to join the Thirlmere aqueduct, so giving an early benefit of water from Haweswater. Bolton took its first supplies via the Thirlmere aqueduct in January 1942. Further delayed by the war, the complete Haweswater pipeline to Manchester was finally commissioned in 1955.

Things did not rest there however, with the Wayoh reservoir being doubled in 1962 and the Jumbles reservoir being constructed between 1967 and 1970. The latter gave a compensating water supply on the Bradshaw Brook which allowed both the Turton and Entwistle and Wayoh reservoirs to be used for drinking water. These two reservoirs continue to supply most of Bolton's drinking water today.

All the statutory undertakings supplying water in north-west England were ultimately brought together to form United Utilities in 1995. Individual towns no longer needed to look at local arrangements alone for their water. Indeed, a major new West East Link Main running from the Liverpool area to Bury allows water to be distributed from both Welsh and Lake District sources across the region according to need, thereby ensuring the reliability of future supplies and allowing the infrastructure to be maintained without cutting supplies.

## DID YOU KNOW?

With the catchment areas for water supply expanding and with the need to avoid expensive water treatment in mind, the council proposed to take powers to close certain footpaths on watersheds above Bolton to protect the water quality. Local people objected strongly to the curtailment of their access to the moors and voted against the idea in a poll on 20th November 1880. The provision was dropped.

## DID YOU KNOW?

The successful use of activated sludge to treat sewage prompted W E Speight, the manager of the Bolton works to propose, probably tongue in cheek, that he could see the time coming when "we shall have Messrs Boots of Nottingham supplying house-holders with compressed tablets of Activated Sludge which will be dropped in the pan, flushed away, and the sewage will arrive at the outfall already purified."

# 4. Trains and Planes

## The Bolton and Leigh Railway

The Bolton and Leigh Railway (the B&LR) was the first public railway to open in Lancashire, receiving the royal assent to Lancashire's first successful Railway Act in 1825, thereby pre-dating the Liverpool and Manchester Railway by two years. It was proposed by William Hulton to take coal from his Westhoughton collieries to market. Other sponsors were drawn from textile manufacturers, bleachers, engineers, brewers, and merchants. They engaged the services of George Stephenson to develop the proposals and it is said that he lodged at Hulton Park for three months while he did so.

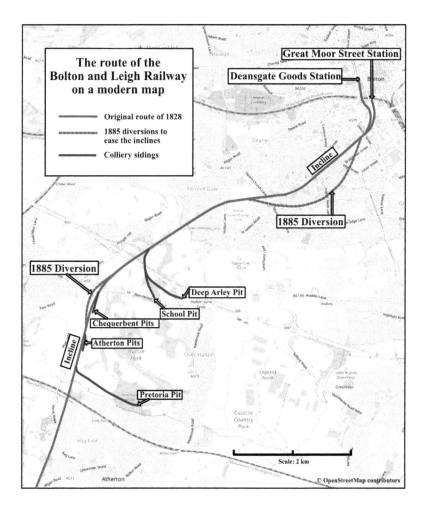

The southern terminus of the line was on the northern bank of the recently opened branch of the Leeds and Liverpool Canal in Westleigh. The Bolton sponsors certainly appreciated that any proposal to cross the canal at that time to make a junction with the proposed Liverpool and Manchester Railway would have been fatal to obtaining the necessary Act of Parliament because of opposition by the canal interests, and they had to be content with a temporary link with the canal instead.

Meanwhile, at the northern end of the line, the original intention had been to terminate the line at the Manchester Bury and Bolton Canal. A fork near the end of the line in Bolton also took a short branch to a goods station on Deansgate (near its junction with Moor Lane). In fact, the route to the canal was cut short to locate its terminus on Great Moor Street. The line down to the canal was never attempted – perhaps due to the severe gradient this would have involved and because of proposals being developed by the MB&B Canal itself to bring a railway from Manchester along the route of its canal.

The railway between Leigh and Bolton had to cross some shallow hills around Chequerbent and it was feared that a steam locomotive would be unable to haul loaded wagons up the necessary gradients. Consequently, cable haulage was decided upon, using stationary engines to draw rolling stock up an incline from Atherton towards Chequerbent and, nearer Bolton, to have an incline running down from Daubhill towards Great Moor Street. The long incline up to Chequerbent with its gradient of 1 in 30 (which became even steeper as subsidence from coal mining in the area took place in later years) made it the steepest in Great Britain used by passenger trains.

The northern section of the line was formally opened from the Hulton colliery near Chequerbent to Bolton on 1 August 1828. The fine weather encouraged perhaps 40,000 to 50,000 people to jostle for a view, many of whom sat on the roofs of factories and houses. The celebrations began soon after noon and Robert Stephenson's steam locomotive built to operate the line was named the *Lancashire Witch* by William Hulton's wife, Maria. The events included trial runs with the locomotive during which speeds of up to 12 mph were achieved. The official party of 120 ladies and gentlemen then travelled down the incline to Bolton at 4 p.m. with the Bolton Old Band playing and flags flying. On the way down the pressure of people waiting to see the procession was so great that at one point three men were thrown into the path of the passing wagons, passing over them and injuring one severely. Having arrived at the bottom of the incline the plan was to draw the wagons to the terminus by horses, although people in the crowd insisted on hauling the wagons themselves. Afterwards the official party enjoyed a 'cold collation' at the Commercial Hotel on the Market Square (now Victoria Square).

In 1831 an extension to the B&LR was opened to Kenyon to make a junction with the Liverpool and Manchester line. This gave the textile manufacturers of Bolton a ready access to the cotton imported through the port at Liverpool as well as a somewhat circuitous route to Manchester. Although the whole line had originally been conceived as a freight-only arrangement, passenger traffic very soon followed, and 40,000 people were reported to have gathered to see the first official passenger service in Bolton on 13 June 1831. To begin with there was only one public station provided along the line, apart from the termini, near Chowbent. However, a halt was also provided near Chequerbent for the personal use of Mr and Mrs Hulton.

BOLTON

ARMS OF BOLTON

REFERENCE.

*Opposite*: Piggot's map of 1824 annotated to show the tentative route of the B&L Railway in yellow.

*Right*: All that remains of the entrance gate to the former railway goods building on Deansgate.

*Below*: A drawing of the *Lancashire Witch* locomotive. (Alexandre Deghilage)

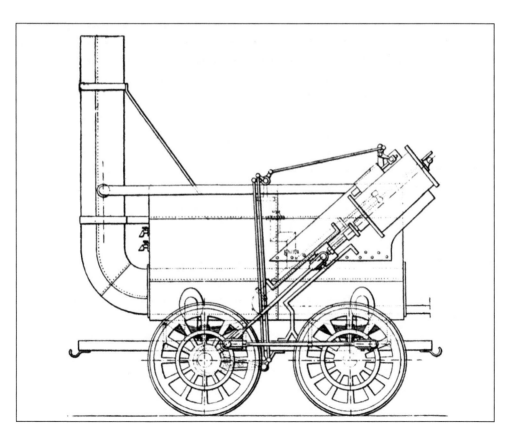

Following the famous Rainhill locomotive trials on the Liverpool and Manchester Railway in 1829 the B&LR leased the near-winning locomotive *Sans Pareil* as a helpmate to the *Lancashire Witch* and it gave good service until 1844, from which point it was used to power a pumping engine at Coppull Colliery in Chorley. Eventually rescued and restored by John Hick of Bolton, *Sans Pareil* was given to the Science Museum and can be seen today at the Shildon Locomotion Museum. A third locomotive named *Union* was also built for the line and delivered in 1830. Designed and built by John's father Benjamin Hick, this was the first of around 230 locomotives produced at the Union Foundry of Rothwell, Hick and Rothwell in Bolton. Their exports subsequently went around the world, and particularly to America.

The immediate effect of the opening of the B&LR was a reduction in the price of coal in Bolton (said to be worth the same as if all assessed taxes on manufacturing had been

Looking towards Bolton on the B&L Railway from the Rothwell Street overbridge, 1960s. (Paul Salveson)

repealed). There was a great business opportunity linked to the operation on the railway as well and, in the early days, John Hargreaves of Hart Common Farm in Westhoughton saw that potential. He already operated as a local carrier of goods and it was not long before he obtained the running rights on the B&LR and other rights to operate trains to Liverpool. John and his engineer son William were subsequently offered the chance to join John Hick to become partners in the Soho Ironworks in Bolton which had been established in 1833 by Benjamin Hick after he left the Union Foundry. Later, when John Hick retired from active management on being elected as a Bolton MP in 1868, William took on the overall management and renamed the firm as Hick, Hargreaves & Co. Both Hick's Soho Ironworks and the Union Foundry in Bolton continued to build railway locomotives during the 1840s and 1850s alongside their general millwrighting and construction of stationary steam engines for mills.

The B&LR was amalgamated into the Grand Junction Railway in 1845 and then, soon after, into the London and North Western Railway. The two rope-hauled inclines were finally dispensed with in 1885 when a double-track diversionary line was opened around Chequerbent and down to Bolton from Daubhill. The use of the line diminished after 1930 when the Pretoria Colliery closed and the final closure for passengers (except for excursions) came in 1954. Freight services were withdrawn in sections between 1963 and 1969 and the line abandoned. However, it is still possible to see evidence of the original alignment at a few points today.

The Chequerbent incline on the B&L Railway today.

## DID YOU KNOW?

It has been suggested that while living at Hulton Park, George Stephenson took the chance to have writing lessons from the village schoolmaster alongside William Hulton's sons. This seems very unlikely given that George was the author of many letters and reports to his railway clients. However, if true that would be a most interesting sidelight on the skills of a very competent civil engineer.

## DID YOU KNOW?

In the early days a means of signalling the driver of the stationary engine at the top of the Daubhill incline was needed to indicate when things were ready to haul wagons up the slope. The simple expedient of placing a spanner on top of the rope at the summit was followed. Then, when haulage was to begin, the wagons at the bottom were pulled back a short distance causing the spanner to fall, giving the requisite signal to the engineman.

## Bolton's Gentleman Aviator

While still a junior at Bolton school in 1908 John Scott Taggart founded the Bolton Aero Club and, with another boy, built a model of Farman's biplane for the Hobbies Exhibition of 1910. Although he never lost his fascination with aviation he quickly moved on to radio and was soon transmitting messages from one part of the school grounds to another.

On leaving school during the First World War he joined the army, serving in various units including the 55th (West Lancashire) Infantry Division. He did well. He was mentioned in dispatches and awarded the Military Cross for his radio work during the fourth Battle of Ypres when the Germans mounted their spring offensive of April 1918.

Back as a civilian, John married Dorothy Jefferson in December 1920 and started a career as a talented radio engineer. He became the youngest member of the British Institute of Physics in 1921 and, while working with the Radio Communication Company in 1922, founded Radio Press Ltd and wrote many books for the amateur radio enthusiast. Sales eventually topped 750,000 volumes. He edited *Modern Wireless* and *Wireless Weekly* and wrote a weekly column for the *Daily Express*. During the 1920s more than 100,000 amateurs built their own radio sets based on his designs, helping to establish the popularity of the early BBC broadcasts.

He eventually sold his publication business to the Amalgamated Press in 1926 and became qualified as a barrister in 1928, although he never practised as such. Instead he decided to learn to fly and live the life of a gentleman aviator. He obtained his Royal Aero Club Aviator's Certificate on 19 January 1929 flying a De Havilland 60 Moth aircraft. By

John Scott Taggart, 1929.

this time, he was obviously a wealthy and generous man, donating a Gipsy Moth aircraft to the London Aeroplane Club in May 1929.

For his own use he bought another Gipsy Moth biplane and, in February 1929, with only five or six hours' solo flying experience, undertook a successful flying tour to Lausanne in Switzerland. Very soon after his return to England in April 1929 he flew solo to Bolton for the wedding of his sister-in-law, Miss Winifred Jefferson, where he intended to land in a field off Markland Hill Lane. Owing to a misunderstanding with the man who had been designated to indicate the wind direction for the landing, John was obliged to remain in the air in order not to run the man down. Unfortunately, he could not clear the trees at the end of the field and the aircraft hit the topmost branches at around 50 or 60 mph. It descended nose first into the kitchen garden next to No. 123 Markland Hill Lane. He was fortunate to suffer no more than bruises and a broken rib. Naturally, he attended the wedding.

Later that year he made a prolonged visit to the USA and, at the same time, his aircraft was rebuilt. When it flew again, it was as an amphibious plane, fitted with both floats and wheels by Short Brothers. He used it at the Cinque Ports Flying Club near his home in Hythe and visited the 1929 Schneider Trophy competition for high-speed float planes that September. While there he flew from the Solent and his aircraft was to be seen moored alongside the steam yacht *Conqueror*, owned by Harry Gordon Selfridge of department store fame.

John Scott Taggart's Gipsy Moth with the house on Markland Hill Lane behind. (*Sheffield Daily Telegraph*)

The house on Markland Hill Lane today.

The garden where the Gipsy Moth descended.

On Christmas Eve 1929, while flying with his twenty-two-year-old brother-in-law Sidney Jefferson as passenger, John attempted a landing on the sea in the Channel a mile off Sandgate, near Folkestone. Caught by a large wave the aircraft turned upside down, leaving the two flyers clinging to the plane's upturned float. They were eventually rescued, bruised, wet and cold, but otherwise unhurt, by Harry Wire (a well-known Hythe footballer) and 'Sonny' Griggs in a rowing boat from Hythe. They had grabbed the first boat on the beach when they saw the aircraft ditch and pressed on with the rescue despite the boat having had its plugs withdrawn. They were eventually rowing up to their knees in water. On regaining dry ground, the flyers caught a bus back to John's home. They must have looked a fair sight. Meanwhile the abandoned aircraft was wrecked when it was washed up at Folkestone on Christmas Day. John was later asked if it was true that all one's past sins float before one's eyes just before a crash. He replied 'No – either there are no sins or there is no time.'

He was soon up and running again, determined to overcome the shock by flying to Bolton two days later in his second aircraft. He also set off on new adventures, including another winter tour of Europe in early 1930. By 1932 he had owned five aircraft in quick succession and had had three narrow escapes.

Early in 1932 he published a novel, *The First Commandment*, as a whimsical divertissement which was well received. That same year he returned to wireless

An advert for the floatplane conversion featuring John Scott Taggart's aircraft. (www.aviationancestry.co.uk)

journalism with the Amalgamated Press, resuming his design of radio sets for the home constructor, hundreds of thousands more sets being made.

With the outbreak of Second World War John joined up again, this time with the Royal Air Force. He served in France in 1939–40, escaping with his radar unit just before the Dunkirk evacuation. The Germans investigated the transmitter unit left behind and it was on this basis that they formed some of their views about British radar. John subsequently joined the Air Ministry, being responsible for radar training in 1940–41, and became the Senior Technical Officer No. 73 Wing, responsible for radar stations in most of England and Wales between 1943 and 1945.

Later in his service career he was with the Admiralty Signal and Radar Establishment until he retired in 1959. In his retirement years he followed his interest in Italian Majolica pottery and published works on the subject. Awarded the OBE in 1975, John died in Beaconsfield in 1979, a most illustrious Boltonian.

## DID YOU KNOW?

In 1909 Maurice and William Edwards obtained a patent for a two-cylinder horizontal 2-stroke petrol aero engine which dispensed with external pipes by using passages internal to the engine to convey fluids and gases. Several engines were made along these lines at the Bolton Mutual Garage at Byng Street East (at the southern end of Bradshawgate) and powered early aircraft with some success. One purchaser of their engine was James Alcock, later to undertake the first successful flight across the Atlantic in 1919. Maurice Edwards was himself an aviator, flying a Farman biplane at Lancashire air meetings.

## Some Other Aviation Accidents Around Bolton

Even though planned, there has never been a proper aerodrome within the borough to encourage flying. There have nevertheless been several aviation incidents around the town, often linked to bad weather and the high ground of the Anglezarke moors to the north. Perhaps the best-known accident occurred in 1958 when a Bristol Wayfarer airliner crashed near to the television mast on Winter Hill causing thirty-five fatalities, but the emphasis here is on two other, lesser-known events.

Two years into the Second World War Sgt Thomas Blackburn probably wanted to impress his wife, Doris, by flying over their home on the north side of Bolton in his single-seater Curtiss Tomahawk fighter plane of No. 10 Sqn, RAF. However, things did not turn out as he planned. That morning, Friday 17 October 1941, his aircraft crashed into the rear of a house at No. 50 Mornington Road and burst into flames. Luckily no one on the ground was seriously injured although Thomas was killed. Two people were taken to hospital for treatment having been burned trying to rescue the pilot. An octogenarian resident, a Mrs Turner, had a miraculous escape when she was sweeping a carpet in her backyard as the plane struck the back of her home. The fire brigade eventually dragged the wreckage away from the house using ropes and it was later removed for investigation. Although Thomas had over 150 hours' flying experience, he had only flown that fighter type for two of them. His inexperience probably contributed to the accident which was decided later to have been caused by low flying and unauthorised aerobatics, although that was subsequently disputed. Thomas is buried in a war grave in Astley Bridge.

Twelve years later, on Saturday 14 November 1953, two Meteor jet fighter aircraft crashed on the high moors near Edgworth while flying in close formation in drizzling rain and poor visibility, not far from Crowthorn School. They were from 610 (County of Chester) Sqn of the Royal Auxiliary Air Force based at Hooton Park. Wreckage was spread over a square mile and two bodies were recovered. The pilots were Flt Lt Anthony Basil Mercer of Christleton and Flying Officer Arthur Michael Fletcher (aged twenty-four) of No. 9 Mornington Road, Bolton. The Fletchers lived across the road from where Thomas Blackburn had crashed earlier. The Meteor pilots were both weekend flyers although with

*Above*: Mornington Road, where Thomas Blackburn crashed.

*Left*: The house at No. 50 Mornington Road.

great experience. The two men had set out on a weather reconnaissance but changed that to carrying out mock attacks on each other. The reason why they had descended so low is unknown and they crashed at 340 mph while still in formation, punching two adjacent holes in the dry-stone wall where they hit the hill.

# 5. Philanthropy

William Hesketh Lever (later Lord Leverhulme), Andrew Carnegie and the Earls of Bradford are well- known and very generous benefactors associated with Bolton, but this section of the book concentrates on some of the others.

## William Hulme of Kearsley (1631–91)

William Hulme was probably brought up as a child in the Breightmet area and is believed to have attended Brasenose College, Oxford University. His marriage in 1653 brought him an estate and the mansion of Kearsley Hall which was the most significant home

The detached tower of Ringley Church.

in the Kearsley area, having seven of the thirty-nine taxed hearths in the area in 1666. Despite having property elsewhere William lived in Kearsley for most of his life and regularly attended church in Ringley where the minister was supported in part from an endowment of land bought by William. Shortly before he died William also gave money to increase the income of the lecturer at Bolton Parish Church who preached on Fridays and Sundays. The money was used to improve and settle 8 acres of common land on Bolton Moor (Lecturer's Close, south of the town centre) to generate rents for that purpose.

On his death, and having no children, William wished to support scholarships at Brasenose from the income received from his landholdings in Heaton-Norris, Denton, Ashton-under-Lyne, Reddish, Harwood and, more particularly, from his land in Manchester. However, from relatively modest beginnings the income grew until it became a *cause celebre* in the nineteenth century.

His intention was to give an income to four 'poor sort of Bachelors of Arts' who wished to stay in Oxford for four years after taking their first degree to allow them to study for a master's degree. He had in mind scholars originating in the North West so that they may return and provide a high-quality representation for the Church of England at a time when nonconformity was growing in Lancashire.

As Manchester expanded during the Industrial Revolution William's land became some of the most valuable real estate in the country, including Shudehill, Albert Square, Brazennose Street and John Dalton Street. The trustees charged with administering the money found themselves facing an income stream far in excess of anything that William could have envisaged and far in excess of what was needed to provide for William's intentions as expressed in his will. An income of £40 in 1691 had expanded to £5,161 by 1825 and considerable accumulated savings had also been made.

William Hulme's original wishes were of course observed, but what to do with the surplus? Money was offered to Brasenose to create accommodation for the Hulme scholars, but this was turned down since the college did not wish to discriminate between their students in that way. As an alternative the trustees sought the permission of parliament to buy advowsons (the right to place a priest in a parish and give them an income) for former scholars – which some alleged were too often the relatives or friends of the trustees. Unsurprisingly this proved controversial and ran counter to the intentions of the original will in which William had stipulated that the benefit would stop after four years for each scholar. But time had moved on and his original intentions had become obsolete.

Strenuous efforts were made to try to divert the funds into more deserving causes, although it wasn't until 1881 that an Act of Parliament finally remodelled the fund to allow part of the money to be applied more generally to education in the Manchester area. The William Hulme Grammar School, Manchester Grammar School, Manchester High School for Girls, Oldham Hulme Grammar School, Bury Grammar School and Owens College (which would ultimately become part of Manchester University) all benefitted.

What started as a modest bequest has disbursed approximately £20 million since it was founded.

## DID YOU KNOW?

George Piggot was very active in Bolton affairs and suggested ways in which the Earls of Bradford could guide their philanthropy to suit their objectives. He was a Poor Law Guardian for Great Lever and was described as a rigorous economist, keeping the poor rate down by finding employment for paupers. He was elected as an Alderman for the borough in 1844, served on local turnpike trusts and was a churchwarden at the parish church. George later served as a churchwarden at St Michael's Church, Great Lever where his grave can be seen near to the church today.

In the foreground, the grave of George Piggot at St Michael's Church, Great Lever.

## Peter Ormrod (1796–1875)

Peter Ormrod was a partner with Thomas Hardcastle in the company Ormrod and Hardcastle, spinners of Flash Street and Bullfield Mills, just outside Bolton town centre. His father, James, was a founder of the Bolton Bank with four other local businessmen and Peter inherited his father's bank partnership in 1825. He bought 6,000 acres of land in Bowland in 1856 to create his family estate, building Wyresdale Hall at a cost of £50,000 (around £4 million today), designed by the architect Edward Graham Paley of Lancaster.

Bolton Parish Church, possibly at the time of its consecration. (© Bolton Council. From the Collection of Bolton Library and Museum Services)

When Bolton parish church was rebuilt between 1867 and 1871 Peter Ormrod met the whole cost (£40,000) using the same architect. His brother, James, incidentally, built the original St Luke's Church on Chorley Old Road.

## Stephen Blair (1804–70)

In 1826, at the early age of twenty-two, Stephen Blair and his brother Harrison inherited the Mill Hill bleach works on Folds Road from their father. Expansion of the works followed to make Stephen one of the town's wealthiest industrialists. He took Elisha Sumner as a partner after his brother left to concentrate on his chemical works in Kearsley and this gave him time to pursue his interest in public service. Stephen was elected as a borough councillor in 1842 and served as the town's first Conservative mayor in 1845–46. He was a Member of Parliament for Bolton between 1848 and 1852.

Stephen was a prominent Freemason, becoming a member of the Anchor and Hope Lodge in Bolton, and their Worshipful Master in 1835. He rose to be the Provincial Grand Master in 1856 and served in that capacity for fourteen years.

A painting of Stephen Blair wearing Masonic regalia. (David Hawkins)

Philanthropy was obviously particularly important to him. Two churches, the Bolton infirmary, the Workshops for the Blind and the Royal National Lifeboat Institution all benefitted from his generosity, but his most significant gift was a bequest of £30,000 on his death in 1870 to construct and equip a free hospital for sick people 'without limit of domicile'. It took some time to come to fruition, but land was eventually given by another mayor, James Knowles, on what became Hospital Road, Bromley Cross and Blair Hospital was opened in 1887. Like other buildings in Bolton (e.g., Watermillock on Crompton Way) Blair Hospital was used to treat wounded soldiers in the First World War, although for most of its life it operated as a convalescent home. The building closed in 1991 to be subsequently used as an Islamic college, followed by redevelopment for homes by Barratt Developments.

## James Eden (1796–1874)

James Eden was a senior partner in Eden and Thwaites, bleachers at Waters Meeting Works, adjacent to Eagley Brook. His concern was the welfare of children, which led him to found the Eden Orphanage Charitable Trust in 1872. When he died in 1874, he left a comprehensive legacy to complete an orphanage on Thorns Road, Astley Bridge, leaving £10,000 to build the orphanage itself and a further £40,000 to pay for the running costs. He also donated the land.

The former entrance lodge to the Eden Orphanage.

The Eden Orphanage date stone.

Opened in 1879, the orphanage expanded over the years with a school being added in 1884, a gymnasium in 1889 and an infirmary in 1890 (after an outbreak of scarlet fever had necessitated some of the children being cared for in the workhouse and the borough hospital). By 1904 the establishment boasted a small outdoor swimming pool and a museum integral to the school. Children were admitted between the ages of five and sixteen.

Nearly all the buildings have gone today, although the former entrance lodge can still be seen on Thorns Road. Meanwhile the James Eden Foundation continues, offering young people in Bolton (particularly orphans or those with divorced parents) financial assistance towards their further education.

## John Pennington Thomasson (1841–1904)

Born into a family of Quakers, although a Unitarian himself, John Thomasson was elected to represent Bolton in parliament as a Liberal between 1880 and 1885. He was a cotton spinner who ran Mill Hill Mills in the Haulgh. He gave over 100 scholarships and financed the building of the Haulgh Board School in 1881. Overall, he gave over £30,000 towards education in Bolton.

Mere Hall and Park in Halliwell was the subject of a further donation in 1889. The hall, originally built in around 1837 for Benjamin Dobson, was restricted in Thomasson's gift

John Pennington Thomasson on a plaque at the entrance to Mere Hall park.

Mere Hall.

to be used as a building for public benefit. Originally a library, museum and art gallery, the hall was later used as a children's nursery, the Bolton register office, and is now used for the Bolton Music Service. One of John's sons, Franklin, also entered parliament as a Liberal and became involved in the garden city movement which developed Letchworth in Hertfordshire.

### Edmund Peel Potter (1847–1933)
In 1919 Edmund Potter gave his home, Fernclough, on Chorley New Road, to the Bolton Infirmary Committee for use as a convalescent home for women and children. Designed by George Woodhouse in the Gothic style for John Kynaston Cross in the 1860s, the house had been acquired by Edmund Potter in 1899. If the family ever made it their home, it was not for long since it was rented to a colliery agent by 1911 and the Potters had moved to Windermere in the Lake District.

Edmund started his career working for his father as a calico printer but became interested in the dyes used on cloth. Wanting to develop this as a business opportunity he and a partner called Crompton bought an ailing chemical works on Hall Lane, Little Lever and made a success of it, manufacturing the acids and alkalis needed for bleaching cloth. The company's most successful products were sodium and potassium bichromate and these were the source of Edmund's fortune.

*Fernclough.* The former home of Edmund Potter.

After a long period as part of the health service Fernclough survives in magnificent condition today as Ladybridge Hall, acting as a conference centre and the headquarters of the North West Ambulance Service. The former stables adjacent to the hall are now the home of the Bolton Mountain Rescue Team.

## James William Wigglesworth (1875–1966)

The son of a butcher, James Wigglesworth was born near Dewsbury in 1875. He became a pharmaceuticals manufacturer and blossomed as a Bolton benefactor. His company occupied a former silk mill in Westhoughton on the corner of Peel Street and Church Street. One of their successful products was Opas, a stomach digestive tablet and powder produced to a formula prescribed by a Dr Hugh MacLean. (The tablets were a straightforward mixture of calcium carbonate, magnesium carbonate and sodium bicarbonate, but effective nonetheless.) The company seems to have been active in Westhoughton from at least 1917 and they also operated out of Dublin for the Irish market.

In the 1950s James became a benefactor to Bolton. In 1952 he gave a new conservatory in Queen's Park for exotic plants. This was complemented by a 2,000-seat open-air theatre in Moss Bank Park. In March 1956 he gave the Bolton Mayoral Jewel to the then Mayor, Stanley Entwistle. It contains 124 rubies, 18 pearls and 20 diamonds and is intended for evening wear. In 1964 he donated fountains and floodlighting on Victoria Square as well as railings around Queen's Park. He was given the Freedom of the County Borough in 1963. He died in March 1966 while living at High View, Chorley New Road, leaving an estate worth more than £300,000.

## DID YOU KNOW?

In 1840 Elizabeth Lum gave money to build six almshouses for twelve elderly, poor widows or spinsters in Anchor Street, Little Bolton, where they received one shilling a week, with coal, gas and water free of charge. They were eventually demolished for the gasworks on Lum Street and replaced by the borough council in 1886 on Mackenzie Street in Astley Bridge, where they can still be seen, rebuilt in 1920, and appropriately called Mrs Lum's almshouses. Today, the original Anchor Street site is occupied by the Verna Care Ltd factory on Folds Road.

*Above*: Mrs Lum's almshouses, Mackenzie Street.

*Left*: Mrs Lum's almshouses commemorative stone.

# 6. Fresh Air and Fun

## Parks and Gardens

During the early Industrial Revolution Bolton grew into a tightly knit town without much regard for open space. In 1850 Robert Heywood, the bleacher, proposed to counter this by establishing a public park named after Sir Robert Peel. However, the public subscriptions he hoped for did not materialise and the cost of the land also proved prohibitive. The Earl of Bradford declined to make some of his land available, possibly because he disliked the proposed name (unlike Peel, Bradford was an old-fashioned free trade Tory). However, after the Heywood proposal fell, Lord Bradford stepped into the breach in 1854 with the offer of 20 acres for Bradford Park, located in the Haulgh between Radcliffe Road and the River Tonge. The proposal was subject to the council agreeing to pay for the upkeep. The offer was accepted, and the grounds laid out for cricket, football 'and other healthy sports'. The Earl retained ownership of the land and many years later the park was closed. Today the area forms part of the Leverhulme Local Nature Reserve which extends across the river to Leverhulme Park itself.

The Leverhulme local nature reserve, once Bradford Park.

At around the same time in Farnworth, the textile magnate Thomas Barnes MP gave 12 acres for a public park out of his Birch Hall estate. Although the park designer, William Henderson of Birkenhead, was originally engaged to undertake the design and construction, he did not complete the engagement and the task went to Robert Galloway who had been the gardener at Birch Hall. The park was intended to commemorate Barnes's father and mark his son's coming of age. A massive party was planned for the opening on 12 October 1864 and up to 100,000 people witnessed the opening ceremony by the Chancellor of the Exchequer, William Gladstone MP. Streets were decorated with triumphal arches, factories and shops were closed, and people came from far and wide, arriving from 7 o'clock in the morning to witness the 3-mile-long procession and to join the celebrations. However, the correspondent of the *Standard* newspaper could not avoid commenting on the many operatives present who looked gaunt, with 'their wretchedly-clad wives and children whose pallid care-worn countenances bespeak in unmistakable terms the present sad condition of adjacent districts'.

The opening ceremony at Farnworth Park. (Penny Illustrated Paper)

The Barnes memorial in Farnworth Park.

Once again, the local authority was expected to pay for the maintenance and members of the public were required to restrict themselves to activities 'of a quiet nature' with no political or religious meetings, no refreshments and no alcohol. Open-air concerts were given however, with James Barnes (Thomas's son) conducting a brass band. Part of Robert Galloway's reward was to be appointed as park superintendent until he retired in 1895.

During the early 1860s Robert Heywood repeated his offer of land for a park at High Street, Bolton although this was slow to come to completion because of arguments over the need for additional land to be provided at public expense. Meanwhile the council was promoting a much larger Bolton Park (later renamed Queen's Park in 1897) on 46 acres of meadow and pastureland between Chorley New Road and Spa Fields and which was authorised by the Bolton Improvement Acts of 1864 and 1865. The two parks were again designed by William Henderson and the work needed for their construction came at an opportune moment since the town was suffering badly from unemployment caused by the cotton famine linked to the American Civil War.

Both the Heywood and Bolton parks were opened by the Earl of Bradford in May 1866, although he professed to have nothing to do with either in his opening speech. The day was marked by a general holiday and Bolton streets and buildings were decorated with streamers and flags. A procession proceeded from the Market Square to both Heywood and Bolton parks in turn, although none of the trades' societies took part because of a clash with their arrangements for Whitsun. The military and Sunday school children

Heywood Park.

Queen's Park (formerly Bolton Park).

were there in strength, however. The ceremonies were followed by dinner at the Assembly Room over the baths on Lower Bridgeman Street, on which occasion Lieut-Col Gray MP took the opportunity to express the hope that Lancashire would support Cheshire, then afflicted by the cattle plague.

Flower beds, a fountain and a refreshment house were provided in Bolton Park for the pursuit of healthy, moral, and rational pastimes. The park rules prohibited games, noise, drinking alcohol, and bad language. Brass band music was also banned on Sundays. The parks were initially closed on Sunday mornings, although this was challenged within a year. Sunday schools objected to any change on the grounds that they were likely to lose their scholars – important not just for religious observance but for basic learning as well. After a controversial debate it was decided to open the parks. In 1869 the controversy surfaced again when a proposal to sell refreshments on a Sunday was raised. Mayor James Barlow held a public meeting in the Temperance Hall to discuss the matter and around 2,000 men turned up. After a testy debate in which various tactics were used to obscure or interfere with the voting, the decision went in favour of the proposal.

The creation of these open spaces must have been welcome in a town where smoke, pollution and insanitary conditions were the norm, and the River Croal adjacent to Bolton Park was often noisome because of pollution. In fact, the park fountain itself was a failure because of the poor water quality.

Bolton Park was extended across the River Croal in 1875 and other parks and grounds were the subject of private donations during the second half of the nineteenth century: the Darbyshire recreation ground on Slater Street was given by S. D. and C. J. Darbyshire (the first mayor of the borough) in 1868; Mere Hall and the Thomasson Park were given by J. P. Thomasson in 1889; and the 3-acre Bridgeman Park was given by the Earl of Bradford in 1894. In 1913 Great Lever Park was formally opened by the Countess of Bradford.

During the First World War the council opened discussions with Col Richard Ainsworth about the purchase of the 72-acre Moss Bank Estate. This resulted in Moss Bank Park being opened in June 1928. Other land was also acquired at much the same time at Hall i' th' Wood and at Hulton Lane. However, the major acquisition came in September 1938 when the council bought the 2,112-acre Smithills Estate including Smithills Hall itself, and large areas of moorland beyond Scout Road. This was the location for a 'Grand Civic Garden Party' in 1938 to celebrate the centenary of the incorporation of the borough. The Mayor, Alderman Thomas Halstead, invited everyone to join him at Smithills on Saturday 16 and Wednesday 20 July for a lively day out and to inspect the property which was soon to belong to the town. Up to 30,000 people are believed to have attended at 6d a head. The RAF arranged a flypast of heavy bombers, an aquatic display was mounted by the Bolton Swimming Club and Miss Ethel 'Sonny' Lowry described her successful cross-Channel swim of 1933. Among many other attractions were a funfair, cricket matches, a swimsuit beauty parade, a 'health and beauty' demonstration, motorcycle trick riding, and horse jumping. Music was provided by Joe Hill and the Bolton Grand Theatre Orchestra and dancing was enjoyed into the evening.

## DID YOU KNOW?

The park-keeper's cottage which was built on Radcliffe Road at the entrance to the park in the Haulgh eventually became a private residence. For many years it was occupied by Fred Dibnah, the steeplejack. It was there that he established an informal industrial museum and a mock coal mine shaft.

Once the park-keeper's house for Bradford Park and Fred Dibnah's home.

## The Mass Trespass on Winter Hill

The Smithills Estate had been sold to the Ainsworth family in 1801. Richard Ainsworth operated a successful chemical bleaching works in Halliwell, and the important water rights that came with the estate stretched up to Winter Hill. However, on inheriting a share of his father's business in 1833 his eldest son, Peter, decided to live the life of a country gentleman in Smithills Hall, leaving the running of the business to his brother, John Horrocks Ainsworth. Peter took up politics, becoming MP for Bolton between 1837 and 1847. He died in 1870 and the Smithills Estate passed to his nephew Col Richard Ainsworth. Col Ainsworth employed George Devey to remodel Smithills Hall between 1874 and 1884, but when he turned sixty, Richard decided to sell the bleaching business and retire to Winwick Warren in Northamptonshire where he became High Sherriff. Smithills Hall appears to have been used as a home only occasionally after 1900.

In 1896 Col Ainsworth put gates across the road to the moorland above Smithills to protect his shooting rights and employed men to warn off trespassers. This led to a public outcry. In September a considerable number of Boltonians marched up to Winter Hill to protect what they considered to be an ancient right of way.

At that time there was a national movement to preserve the countryside, and access to it, as a counterweight to the polluted and crowded environment of industrial towns. The National Trust for example had been established by Octavia Hill and others in 1895. Direct action to assert the right of access to the countryside had already taken place on Darwen Moor in 1879 and on Latrigg, near Keswick, in 1887. Although many rambling clubs had been established in the nineteenth century, until the later years the pastime was mainly a recreation for the well-off and often involved the danger of being prosecuted for trespass. From the 1880s however a working-class interest in the countryside developed and was often associated with radical politics. The increasing concentration of large areas of land in relatively few hands and its closure to the public led to feelings of injustice and the notion that the land should belong to all the people.

So, when Col Ainsworth took his stand, the Social Democratic Foundation paid for a small advertisement in a Bolton paper inviting all-comers to join in a demonstration on Sunday 6 September 1896 to assert that there was a right of way across Winter Hill. A crowd of around 1,000 collected in the town that morning and, after speeches from William Hutchinson, Joe Shufflebotham and Solomon Partington (a local journalist), marched up Halliwell Road. Many others joined in as the crowd approached the hill, swelling the numbers to around 10,000. Continuing up Smithills Dean Road passing the hall, the crowd reached the moorland where they were confronted by the Colonel's men and a small police contingent. The *Bolton Chronicle* reported that 'amid the lusty shouting of the crowd the gate was attacked by powerful hands ... short work was made of the wooden barrier and with a ring of triumph the demonstrators rushed through into the disputed territory'. Police Inspector Willoughby had to escape by diving over a dry-stone wall and a gamekeeper was ducked in a ditch. The crowd continued to the summit of Winter Hill to enjoy the view and some found their way down to Belmont.

As was often the way, a song was composed, written by the socialist Allen Clarke:

Will yo' come o' Sunday morning,
For a walk o'er Winter Hill?
Ten thousand went last Sunday,
But there's room for thousands still!

O the moors are rare and bonny,
And the heather's sweet and fine,
An' the road across the hilltops,
Is the public's – yours and mine!

The following Sunday another great crowd of 12,000 took up the trespass despite the wet weather, but things were not clarified legally for many years. Many writs were taken out by Col Ainsworth against the ringleaders. Over forty witnesses appeared for the defence at the subsequent trial, but the case was lost. William Hutchinson, Joe Shufflebotham, Matt Phair, Solomon Partington and several others had to face court costs of £600 (perhaps £80,000 in today's money).

It took a further trespass on Kinder Scout in 1932 to trigger the legal right to roam the hills and moorlands. Strangely, the footpath to Winter Hill was not made an official right of way until June 1996, almost a century after the original trespass.

A view across Smithills Moor.

The stone (right) marking the start of the trespass.

The inscription on the stone marking the trespass.

## DID YOU KNOW?

William Hesketh Lever (later Lord Leverhulme) also saw the value of open-air recreation in an industrial town such as Bolton and backed this up with gifts of land for local people to enjoy. He purchased and then gave over 70 acres of land to the town to create Bolton's largest urban park, Leverhulme Park, in 1919, and also gave extensive land at his Rivington estate, including the site of his former home on the hillside, the 'pigeon tower' and a folly based on Liverpool Castle.

*Above*: Bradshaw Brook in Leverhulme Park.

*Left*: Another view of Leverhulme Park.

# 7. Culture

## Early Theatres and the Music Hall

Bolton had a successful local theatre in what became Mawdsley Street as early as 1800 which attracted the cream of county society. The Bolton Bible Society, the Holcombe Hunt and the military all used the premises from time to time. Amateur actors were found on stage, including the borough coroner (John Taylor) who later became a leading teetotaller. Many strongly religious people were prejudiced against theatricals however and the social status of actors was very low. The middle classes began to stay away from the theatre and by 1839 the Mawdsley Street theatre was having to reduce its prices and adjust its programmes to attract a more working-class audience.

When Little Bolton Town Hall opened in 1828 there was an alternative outlet for what were claimed to be 'more rational and decent entertainments' – lectures, lantern slide

A Bolton Theatre playbill of 1832.

shows, recitals and exhibitions. The Temperance Hall on St George's Road followed in 1840 and set out to attract a wider audience by putting on cheaper entertainments. Although designed somewhat like a chapel, the hall differed in that it boasted two boilers of 50 gallons capacity each which could produce enough water in twenty minutes to serve tea for up to 900 people. The water came direct from the Bolton Water Works.

In 1830 the Beer Act allowed beer houses to open, as opposed to fully licensed premises. In response, the traditional venues were forced to find a way of competing and one way was to establish a singing room. A professional musician and perhaps a vocalist were hired, and the audience would sing along, and maybe even provide their own entertainments. The Star Concert Room was opened at the Millstone Inn in Crown Street by Thomas Sharples in 1832 and was perhaps Britain's first music hall. Its success led Sharples to relocate it when he moved to the Star Inn in Churchgate in 1840. The Star not only offered a concert room, but also a museum containing a wide variety of unusual exhibits – waxwork figures in scenarios, erotic *poses plastiques* by the Kirst family, reconstructions of the execution of murderers, a piece of coal containing a toad, and live animals, amongst others. The roof also offered a promenade giving a panorama of the town, complete with a ship's mast.

The attractions at the Star concert hall were many and varied, including acrobats on horses, 'M. Gouffe, the man monkey', 'Wild's Dog Nelson' and the Perkins Patent Steam Gun. In 1845 Thomas Sharples organised a special train from Manchester to bring people to enjoy the museum and a concert, all for the small charge of one shilling.

William Sharples took over the Star Inn from his father in 1850. Meanwhile the 'Old Theatre' in Mawdsley Street, as it became known, was losing out to the newer and popular music halls by the middle of the century. These had themselves evolved from pub singing rooms. Competition became even stronger after the 1843 Theatres Act eased licensing and allowed a semi-permanent Victoria Theatre to be established on land leased from the Corporation. During its short life the Victoria was both popular and profitable, putting on musical productions, sea battle re-enactments and even volcanic eruptions.

The 'Old Theatre' could not compete with Thomas Sharples's Star Music Hall and sold out to the impresario in 1850. Although the theatre was a useful stopgap after the Star burnt down in July 1852, it soon changed hands again and degenerated into poor-grade offerings. Despite further attempts to make use of the theatre, it closed in the early 1860s and the site was acquired for a new County Court building – today converted into the Courthouse Restaurant.

The fire at the Star gutted the building and led to a considerable amount of demolition work. William Sharples engaged a Mr Simcock (who had constructed the building) to take down the eastern wall of the concert room. Things did not go to plan. The wall collapsed suddenly and buried William's uncle Richard as well as a carter who, luckily, had dived under his cart when the alarm was shouted out. Both escaped with minor injuries. However, most of the wall fell on some hovels in the adjacent Wigan Lane. Most of the occupants escaped, although injured, but three people were 'crushed to atoms'. The ten-year-old Nabey Kilgallen and Michael Larkins were both suffocated, the latter while eating his breakfast seated at his fireside.

The site (right) of the original theatre in Mawdsley Street.

The fire put a lot of people out of work. Mr Benfold, the Wizard, lost all his mechanical, chemical and mathematical apparatus, including a splendid camera. The disaster also triggered a campaign by Nonconformists to prevent the renewal of the Star's licence, not least because of its alleged stimulation of 'base passions' among young people on Sundays, and its link to juvenile crime. At first, the Star and the Millstone had their licences taken away, but they were restored after a month in the absence of any complaints from the wider public.

The Star reopened in 1855 and Churchgate soon became something of an entertainment centre. Additional places of amusement were added and altered in ways that are difficult to chronicle. By 1857 there was both a Star Theatre and a Star Music Hall in operation, soon to be joined by the Theatre Royal (which may have been a renaming of the Star Theatre). It is certain that for a while there were two Theatre Royals in Bolton – the one in Churchgate and the other being the former Old Theatre in Mawdsley Street. Both were operated for a time under the management of William Sharples. By 1858 a new museum was also added in the Churchgate complex and the Star Music Hall was eventually renamed as the Museum Music Hall. Rooms and meals were offered for their clientele, indicating more than a local pull for their audiences. The Angel Inn next door was added in 1862 and the whole complex came under the management of James Pitney Weston by around 1870.

Churchgate today. Modern buildings have replaced the theatres.

James Weston decided to emigrate to the United States in 1877 (although he did not actually manage to go) and he sold his Churchgate premises to a Mr Chaplin who defaulted soon afterwards. However, before Weston left, he bought an old cotton mill in Dawes Street and had it converted into the Temple Opera House. With a capacity of 5,000 it was perhaps too large to succeed, and it closed after a couple of years. An attempt to revive it by Charles Majilton followed in 1881 and for a short while it became the venue for spectacular productions exploiting its large size. Disaster occurred in April 1882 when the Temple burnt down and ruined its owner.

By 1882 the Theatre Royal came under its long-term manager, James Fyfe Elliston. The museum was demolished and rebuilt to form the Victoria Variety Theatre, and Joseph Bryan Geoghegan returned to take on the management. He had been a long-standing chairman of music hall acts in the town. Unfortunately an arsonist intervened on Churchgate on 4 January 1888. At least £12,000 of damage was done to the Theatre Royal. The sprinkler system had not operated because of sabotage and the theatre office had been broken into with a pickaxe, although the safe was found later, still intact.

There was a sympathetic response in the town including a benefit put on at the Temperance Hall soon after the fire and, not to be put off, the theatre was rebuilt to the plans of Frank Matcham in an amazing twenty-week period. The foundation stone was laid by the actor Henry Irving and the theatre reopened the following November with a 'powerful drama' by Henry Pettitt entitled *Hands Across the Sea*. James Elliston had met

*Right*: James Fyfe Elliston, theatre manager.

*Below*: A typical act performed at the Victoria Variety Theatre. (Pictorial News)

Frank Matcham in 1886 when he had asked him to reconstruct parts of the Theatre Royal in Blackburn (another of Elliston's theatres).

Decorated in the Moorish style, the new Bolton Theatre Royal had a smaller capacity (2,500) than previously, but Matcham had conjured up a building with a sumptuous

Frank Matcham, theatre architect.

interior in a very short space of time. Musical comedies and Gilbert and Sullivan became the typical fare. Matcham incidentally had a long career as a theatre architect during which he designed more than ninety venues across the country from 1879, including the London Palladium and the Blackpool Tower Ballroom.

He was active in Bolton again in 1894 when Churchgate witnessed the opening of the Grand Circus of Varieties. The Grand was constructed in the Italianate style, with decorations of a French renaissance character, and could seat 3,000 people. As the name suggests, it had a stage which could be transformed into a sunken circus ring and was used by equestrian acts, dogs and a trapeze artist at the grand opening event, although the circus arrangement seems to have been little used afterwards.

The advent of the Grand soon led to the closure of the Victoria Variety Theatre in 1896 and its refurbishment as a bijou theatre, again to the designs of Frank Matcham. In 1912 the Victoria became a picture house – the Princess Picture Hall – which lasted until 1928 when the shell of the building was incorporated into the rebuilding of the Theatre Royal.

Another music hall appeared in August 1908 when the Empire Theatre of Varieties opened on Deansgate. In 1916 the theatre was renamed the Hippodrome and became a cinema until the early 1940s when it became the home of the Bolton Repertory Theatre. Described as architecturally 'hideous' by Nikolaus Pevsner, closure came in 1961, to be followed by demolition to make a car park. Meanwhile the Theatre Royal had been rebuilt once more and reopened in November 1928 as a theatre and cinema, managing to carry on until its closure in 1962. The Grand had closed as a live theatre in 1960 and despite a

The Octagon Theatre undergoing its latest rebuild.

short spell as a cabaret theatre and bingo hall both the Grand and the Theatre Royal were demolished in September 1963.

Professional theatre did not abandon Bolton in the longer term however with the building of the Octagon Theatre on Howell Croft South, opened by Princess Margaret in November 1967.

## DID YOU KNOW?

On a notorious morning in 1844, the keeper of the menagerie and museum at the Star, Matthew Ferguson, went to look after his animals, but did not reappear after two hours. His assistant found his hat and coat in their normal place, but Ferguson himself was lying dead in the den of Barney the leopard, literally weltering in his blood, having been mangled about the throat and his scalp almost torn off. The proprietor, Thomas Sharples, had the animal stuffed and added to the museum's attractions.

## The Bleackley Family Bijou Orchestra

James Bleackley, born in 1848, established the Bleackley Family Bijou Orchestra. He had been orphaned at the age of ten and had little or no chance to nurture his gift for music. Married to Mary Jane Woolam in 1869, his family extended to two daughters and six sons. While still employed in the textile industry as a spindle and fly maker he studied the violin from the age of twenty-five under Thomas Crompton. A strict family regime of music practice led to the formation of his orchestra and success in the 1890s. The orchestra consisted of James and his six sons, playing piano, violin, cornet, trombone, piccolo, and drums with James on the double bass. They performed for charitable institutions in Bolton such as the Infirmary and the Chadwick Orphanage as well as at the Albert Hall and for family parties. They also travelled to perform. In November 1893 for example they appeared at the Todmorden Comic Carnival on behalf of the Miners' Relief Fund and performed alongside Mr Oscar Kelmere, the laughing king, Mr E. K. Clegg, the paper manipulator and Mr W. Memory, the farmyard mimic. It was reported in the *Todmorden News* that some of the items were not well appreciated! The Bijou Orchestra's wide repertoire included selections from the operas, the classics and dance music and was surely one of the better offerings that day.

### DID YOU KNOW?

A change in theatre audience behaviour was detected by the *Bolton Chronical* on 22 November 1851. Previously, audiences had been quick to applaud a good actor immediately. However, the previous Saturday, during a performance of *Hamlet*, 'scarcely a hand could be heard except at the close of the act; all was quiet as if the actors had been amusing themselves by playing to empty benches'. The newspaper correspondent thought this somewhat unwise. 'An actor requires to be told that he is pleasing; he requires stimulating, urging on; and often needs an interregnum creating by applause that he may take breath, and nerve himself for further efforts.'

# 8. This Sporting Life

## A Day at the Races – Horwich Racecourse

The horse was of course the pre-eminent beast of burden essential to support the progress of both war and commerce until the modern era. Given its key role, it is hardly surprising that people have taken considerable interest in the breeding, keeping and competitive display of the animals. Horse racing is believed to have been practised in England since Roman times, although the sport really received a boost when English knights returned from the Crusades bringing Arab horses with them. Annual horse fairs were natural places to mount competitions and, at the other end of the social scale, many royals were proud owners of racing stables and studs.

Organised horse racing took place in the sixteenth century at Chester, Leith and Doncaster and James I promoted Newmarket in 1605. Despite an interlude during the Commonwealth period, race meetings became more formalised and widespread during the seventeenth century with bets being placed by the crowd. Royal Ascot was founded by Queen Anne in 1711 and some race meetings became important social as well as sporting occasions. The Jockey Club was established in 1750 and soon set out a comprehensive set of rules for meetings and races.

Interest in horse racing reached a peak during the eighteenth and nineteenth centuries, and many entrepreneurs tried their hand at establishing courses and meetings. This included a course at Horwich which seems to have moved around at first, with references being made to meadows behind the Squirrel public house at the bottom of Scholes Bank and a field adjoining Anderton Hall. The first meeting was held in August 1837 and the races were active for eleven years. The principal races included the Manchester Handicap (over 1½ miles), the Horwich Tradesmen's Gold Cup (over 2¼ miles) and the Willoughby Stakes (over 2 miles).

On 1 August 1840 the *Bolton Chronicle* was celebrating the success of the races on the previous Thursday with 'the warmth of summer rays just cooled with gentle breezes' and the grandstand speedily filling by half-past one. 'The site of the course is excellently chosen, being situated amidst some sweet scenery at the foot of Rivington Pike.' Refreshments were served on the course by Mr and Mrs Mascall of the Lever Arms Hotel and the Horwich pubs of the Crown, the Bull, the Beehive and the Horwich Moor Gate all did good trade. 'Everything went off well throughout, especially the provisions, which vanished marvellously.'

In May 1841 the Clerk of the Course, Mr T. Lees, announced the arrangements for the forthcoming races. Outlining five major races over two days in August he claimed that the course would be in 'slap up' condition, weather permitting. The popularity of the races may be judged by the fact that for the races that year, seven special trains were run each day by the Bolton and Preston Railway from Bolton Trinity Street station to Horwich

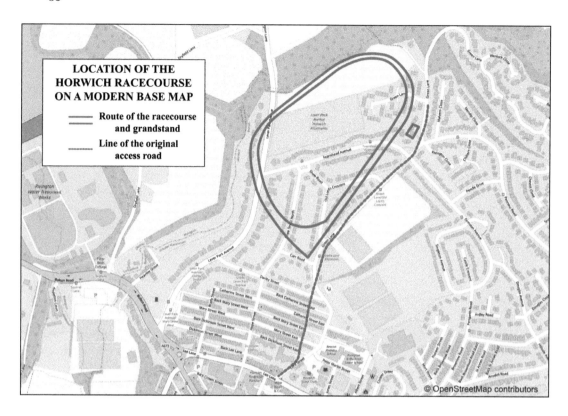

The corner of Green Lane and Pennine Road where the grandstand once stood.

Road station (now Blackrod) for a fare of 1s 6d (first class) or 8d (third class). Two coach proprietors and a farmer were brought to court in Bolton just over a week later for taking paid passengers to and from the races without proper licence arrangements.

By the time the 1847 Ordnance Survey map was produced the course was located on the opposite bank of the River Douglas from where Rivington and Blackrod High School stands today. The site is now crossed by Lever Park Avenue. This was probably the new Crown course for sprint races (and named for the local pub) which held the Willoughby Stakes in 1846, won by Mr Walker's horse, The Nobbler. How many people realise when travelling along Green Lane, near its junction with Pennine Road, that they are on the spot where grandstand crowds cheered the horses and riders over 170 years ago?

## DID YOU KNOW?

Jack 'peg-leg' Isherwood was a celebrated Bolton orange merchant with a wooden leg who took part in a walking race in October 1835 over a 4-mile course. His opponent was Joe Whittle, a weaver from Tottington, who also 'rejoiced in a wooden understanding'. The race took place along Chorley New Road and was observed by around 3,000 people who braved the 'pelting of the pitiless storm'. Around thirty other 'timber toed' men also attended, most of whom had 'thrown a leg at the enemies of old England'. Jack persevered to the end but was beaten by nearly a quarter of a mile.

## Football

Versions of football had been played in Bolton, as elsewhere, well before 1800. Games would take place on holidays and festivals when the whole town became the focus of large disorganised teams fighting for the ball. A veteran local character called Parson Folds often launched games from the yard of the Swan Inn in Bradshawgate and, despite the County Court declaring the games to be a public nuisance in 1791, the games continued into the nineteenth century. Eventually the Highways Act of 1835 prohibited the playing of football on the road with fines of up to 40s imposed on anyone caught.

A little later, the park donated by the Earl of Bradford in the Haulgh in 1854 included football pitches and is likely to have been the home of Haulgh Albion. The growth of the game was helped by the spread of the Saturday half-holiday among textile workers following the Factory Act of 1850 and both churchmen and those brought up in the public school tradition advocated football as a healthy, rational, and character-building recreation. Churches, employers, and public houses were important in the development of the game which was straightforward to play or watch, and which required little in the way of expensive equipment to take part.

The first organised club in the Bolton area was at Turton. The club was founded in 1872 by two sons of James Kay of Turton Tower who had learned to play while at Harrow school. The club was helped by the local schoolmaster (W. T. Dixon) and was viewed as a way to improve the working classes, with membership being restricted initially to members of the local reading room and institute. Members enrolled for one shilling each. A Turton man who later became prominent, John James Bentley, played for the club in its early days and became captain during the 1881–82 season.

With its success, the Turton club soon decided to make payments to some of its players since working men were not able to play on a strictly amateur basis given that they could not afford to spend time training. This became a controversial issue when the club helped found the Lancashire Football Association in 1878 which was proposed initially as an amateur body. John Bentley became secretary and treasurer of the Turton club and represented them on the Lancashire FA. He also took up reporting on matches and eventually joined the staff of *The Athletic News* in the 1880s where he rose to be the editor and remained in post until 1900. Meanwhile he was appointed as Secretary to Bolton Wanderers in 1885 and became a Football Association Councillor in 1888. In 1893 he became President of the League and eventually, Chairman of Manchester United in 1908.

Bolton Wanderers themselves had church origins, started by the Revd Joseph Farrall Wright as the Christ Church Football Club in 1874. Christ Church was located on Blackburn Street (now Deane Road) where the Christ Church gardens and Bolton University are located today, opposite Bolton College. For a while the vicar was the club's president and the church schoolmaster (Thomas Ogden) acted as captain.

Membership of the club was available for one penny a week and games were initially played on a public park, although more formal arrangements were eventually found

The football pitch at Turton today.

Across Deane Road are the gardens where Christ Church was located.

at Pike's Lane, further along what is now Deane Road. The change of name to Bolton Wanderers came about in 1877 when the vicar objected to the club holding its meetings in Christ Church school while he was not there. The 'Wanderers' element reflected the fact that the club had found it difficult to settle on a permanent ground during its first years.

In 1888 the club was one of the twelve founder members of the Football League. (Four other founder members were also from cotton towns.) The League came into being because a group of clubs felt that the great number of cup competitions being organised in the 1880s had tended to produce unpopular games caused by sides being very badly matched in terms of their ability.

Playing on a Saturday afternoon had allowed spectators to be charged for entry (unlike Sundays) and the growing income meant that clubs could employ more professional players, particularly during the 1880s. Professional players, often from Scotland, meant that entertaining matches could be put on for appreciative crowds. The cotton producing areas of Lancashire and Sheffield were in the forefront of this commercialised professional football. Of the one hundred clubs in the second round of the 1883 FA Cup, twenty-five were from south-east Lancashire, including three from Bolton, one from Eagley and one from Turton. After much argument the Football Association agreed to recognise professional players in July 1885, although they were not allowed to play in a cup match unless they were born or lived for two years within 6 miles of the ground or headquarters of the club for whom they wished to play.

The rules of football were agreed between the English, Irish, Scottish and Welsh Football Associations in 1882 when there was final agreement on the size of the ball to be used, the need for clearly marked touchlines, the correct procedure for throwing the ball in from touch, and the need for fixed crossbars as opposed to tapes.

The bigger matches were quite a local event. As an example, the crowd for the Wanderers' cup tie with Notts County in 1884 overflowed the ground at Pike's Lane and around 4,500 people paid local farmers a reduced rate to watch from their fields. A court case later launched by a farmer to claim damages for trampled crops failed ignominiously when it was revealed that he had taken money from the spectators. Some matches were notable for the disruption that occurred during and after the game. In September 1883, Sam Ormerod, the referee of a Wanderers v. Darwen game, was assaulted on his way back to the station from Pike's Lane. Similarly, in January 1884 the referee of a Great Lever v. Preston North End game (Mr Fitzroy Norris) reported he was 'cursed and sworn at by a body of dirty low blackguards ... [and] after the affair was over I was tackled by a flock of infuriated beings in petticoats supposed to be women ... [one of whom] struck me on the back with her gingham and invited the dirty nosed little rascals, who spoil every football match they go to, to crush me'.

The larger clubs which attracted substantial crowds from their hinterlands began to improve their grounds during this decade. They also benefitted from the growing disposable incomes of their predominantly working-class spectators. The Bolton Wanderers balance sheet for 1884–85 shows receipts of £1,949, over 80 per cent of which was obtained from the entrance gates. Interestingly, the accounts show nothing for players' wages although it is almost certain that they were being paid by that time. Out-of-town clubs like Turton were unable to keep up, and after paving the way for modern football, ended up in the Lancashire Combination League founded in 1891–92.

The former Burnden Park football ground seen from the air in 1989.

Reliance on the ground at Pike's Lane changed in 1895 when the Wanderers' new ground at Burnden was opened. Back in 1882 the Gas Department of the council had taken over a large portion of the former waste water treatment plant at Burnden for a new works. However, the gasworks were never proceeded with and in July 1894 Bolton Wanderers negotiated a fourteen-year lease for the site. They stayed for much longer of course.

The *Athletic News* in 1909 noted that 'the vast majority of gentlemen who are pecuniarily interested in [football] clubs look upon their financial obligations as of secondary importance to the sport they get ... thousands have helped create clubs by taking shares without hope of seeing their money back or any return for it'. The strange world of football finance is not just a modern phenomenon.

## DID YOU KNOW?

An American, Sam Scott was a daredevil who jumped into water from great heights. In the States he was notorious for having made a 600-foot leap below Niagara Falls. In January 1838 he came to Bolton and proposed to jump from the Old Quay Company warehouse at the canal wharf. The police turned up and demanded he come down, at which Sam shouted, 'Oh yes, I'm coming', and leapt into the water! Sad to say, in 1841, Scott's last feat was to mount a mock execution of himself while suspended under Waterloo Bridge in London. Twice he cheated the noose, but on the third display his luck ran out and he really did hang himself.

## Cyril Butler Holmes

Born and living in Bolton all his life, Cyril Holmes was an outstanding sportsman who represented England in both athletics and rugby. During the 1930s he was one of Britain's top sprinters and broke records in both the 100- and 220-yard events. He attended Hitler's infamous Berlin Olympics in 1936 but was eliminated in the quarter-finals of the 100 metres because of a torn muscle and was forced to watch from the sidelines as Jesse Owens took the gold medal. However, in 1937 he won the AAA 100 yards in 9.9 seconds at the World University Games.

In 1938 he won twenty-four of his twenty-seven races at the British Empire Games at the Sydney Cricket Ground in Australia, setting a record for the 220 yards in the semi-final which he broke again in the final. The record stood until 1958. He also led the 100-yards race from the start to take the gold medal, although at the finish he ran into a fence, slightly injuring his wrist. Then, in 1939 he won the AAA 220 yards in a time of 21.9 seconds.

During the second World War Cyril joined the Royal Artillery but soon transferred to the Army Physical Training Corps where he served as an instructor at the Royal Military College, Sandhurst. After the war he concluded his international athletics career in a match against France in 1945 and took up rugby union. He was capped three times by England in the 1947–48 season, playing on the wing, scoring a try on

The former home of Cyril Butler Holmes on Stapleton Avenue.

his debut in the Calcutta Cup at Twickenham against Scotland in front of a crowd of 60,000.

Cyril worked for the firm of Thomas Moscrop & Co. Ltd where his father Arthur was managing director. The Holmes family had been associated with the company, which owned the Lion Oil Works on St George's Street, since Mr T. Holmes had made a partnership with Thomas Moscrop in 1864. Moscrops specialised in lubricating oils and were dry salters and manufacturing chemists. Cyril described himself as a traveller in 1939 but in due course rose to be a director. Said to be a real gentleman, he was a member of the Bolton Rotary Club where he served as their president. In 1952 the Holmes family bought Glaisdale, a lovely art deco house on Stapleton Avenue, Heaton. In recent years the home has been sold of course, although a sympathetic rebuild has retained its essential character.

## DID YOU KNOW?

Thomas Horsefall from Ashton made a wager in September 1841 that he could undertake a curious challenge. He bet that he could undertake five tasks within one hour – to gather fifty peas laid 1 yard apart, to run a mile with a hoop, to run half a mile in a sack, to walk a mile and to run a mile. The contest took place in a field near Deane church and was completed in less than thirty-six minutes.

# 9. Making the Modern Town

The coordinated planning of Bolton, laying out streets in advance of development, began with the 1792 Enclosure Act authorising Bolton Moor to be divided into streets and building plots. Similar plans were made in the area of the Haulgh. During the nineteenth century this kind of action continued, as first the trustees of Great and Little Bolton organised urban squares, and then the Corporation carried out several highway widenings, slum clearances and redevelopments to improve the town. A notable example was the clearance of slums north of Deansgate in 1850 to allow the creation of Knowsley Street, with its bridge across the River Croal to connect with St George's Road, and the creation of the Market Hall, completed in 1855. The high-level Marsden Road bridge was also completed at this time.

The Bolton-born entrepreneur William Lever (later Lord Leverhulme) had a strong interest in town planning, having founded the school of Civic Design at Liverpool University in 1909. In 1910 he asked Thomas Mawson to advise on the planning of Bolton. Mawson had already developed proposals for William Lever at Port Sunlight on the Wirral and went on to create many more, including proposals for Calgary in Canada in 1914.

Mawson gave a series of six lectures to the Bolton Housing and Town Planning Society and published a book in 1916 which pointed to the defective layout of Bolton. He was

*Above left*: Marsden Road where it bridges St Helena Road.

*Above right*: A painting of Lord Leverhulme wearing his Masonic regalia. (David Hawkins)

appalled by the slum conditions people were enduring and proposed improvements in line with the garden city movement. He suggested 'green fingers' reaching into the town and small gardens and squares in the town centre. He asked Robert Atkinson to produce several sketches to illustrate his proposals to rearrange streets in the town centre and across the River Croal towards Queen's Park, where a magnificent museum would be located. There was only passing consideration about the precise cost of it all, the benefits being considered as self-evident in terms of improved efficiency, increased rental incomes and lower running costs.

After the First World War, in 1924, Lord Leverhulme returned to these ideas and suggested they be taken up by the council, offering to pay £100,000 towards the cost himself. The offer was politely turned down, probably because it would have been prohibitively expensive even with the donation. Five years later the council produced a Town Planning Scheme for the whole borough which allocated areas for different kinds of development and suggested new roads that could be usefully constructed – including an approximate line for what became Beaumont Road on the western side of the town. The Housing and Town Planning Act of 1919 had made local authorities responsible for the provision of 'working class housing' and by the beginning of the Second World War around 4,000 homes had been built in Bolton. During the same period and partly to alleviate unemployment, the council went ahead with plans to extend Bolton's civic centre to create what is now known as Le Mans Crescent, and which had its official opening in June 1939.

Lord Leverhulme's plan for the area around the market hall on Bridge Street. (Robert Atkinson)

SLIDE NO. 16.—THE CAUSEWAY IN QUEEN'S PARK.

Lord Leverhulme's vision for Queen's Park. (Robert Atkinson)

Beaumont Road. Sometimes said to have been the last A-road in the country to have a surface made of setts.

Following the Second World War, town planning was put on a stronger footing by the 1947 Town and Country Planning Act. Local authorities were required to produce development plans and Turton Urban District Council had an optimistic plan ready for publication that year. This included a completely new town centre for Bromley Cross and a substantial length of a new ring road around the north side of Bolton (neither of which came to fruition). Bolton's own Development Plan was approved in 1952 proposing substantial housing clearance and new housing areas at Breightmet and Ladybridge. The idea of relocating Bolton residents from slum clearance areas to Leyland or Chorley was rejected however as 'unwarranted violation of the freedom of the individual'. Proposals to expand Westhoughton for Salford and Manchester 'overspill' were also abandoned after a public inquiry in 1966, although the town became a major expansion area in the 1970s – but for private housing.

The pressure was on to protect the open land around the borough by the creation of a Green Belt, but this had to await the establishment of the Greater Manchester Council and its Green Belt Local Plan, approved in 1984. In a complementary action, the reclamation of derelict industrial areas went ahead, and plans were also made for the environmental improvement of the Croal/Irwell Valley, including the creation of the Moses Gate country park.

By the early 1960s Bolton's town centre was visibly ageing and at risk of losing its status as a sub-regional centre. A major planning application for shops, offices, a bowling

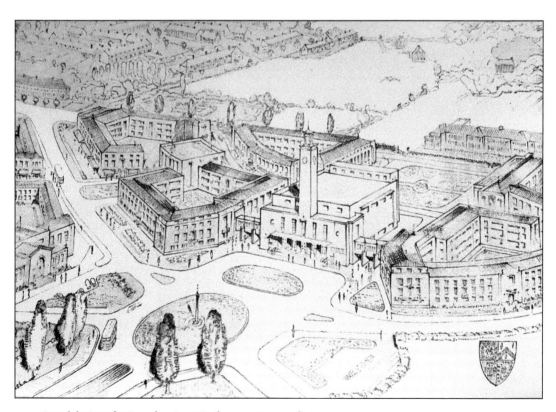

Grand designs for Bromley Cross in the 1947 Turton Plan.

The reservoirs at Moses Gate Country Park.

Rock Hall in Moses Gate Country Park. Once a visitor centre with a ranger service.

alley and skating rink was proposed on land north of the Market Hall by Metrolands Investments Ltd in 1963 but was eventually rejected as being premature pending a look at the wider arrangements.

Seeking to put some shape to those wider arrangements, the council engaged the services of Shankland Cox and Associates to come up with a comprehensive plan, which was approved as the Town Centre Map in August 1965. This proposed a major revision to the layout of the centre with radical new highway arrangements. It identified several areas ripe for redevelopment, organised around a north – south spine of Knowsley Street and Newport Street. The area around the Market Hall was identified as an opportunity for a new landmark development, and it was proposed that the Ashburner Street Market should be moved to the north of the Market Hall. Entertainment and recreational facilities were particularly identified as another requirement, including a new civic theatre, art gallery, bowling alley, ice-skating rink and swimming pool. The plan became a major focus for discussions with private and public developers and ultimately, after a long gestation, led to the Market Place development. Meanwhile, Shankland's suggestions for a new theatre led to the Octagon being opened in 1967. The initial pedestrianisation of the town centre followed in 1969 and the Arndale Centre (later named the Crompton Place) in 1971.

The Shankland Cox proposals were looked at again with the publication of the Town Centre Map Review in 1975 to guide development up to 1991. This confirmed and expanded the eventual need for more retail space, particularly to include a national department store (in the event, Debenhams). It also sought to establish the town centre as an important office location, particularly around the station – something which did not materialise. The Ashburner Street retail market was still to be relocated near to the Market Hall, but now on the other side of Knowsley Street – another ambition which did not come about. Car parking space for 10,000 vehicles was proposed, although even this was thought to be inadequate. A new bus station was suggested spanning Great Moor Street and the pedestrianisation was to be extended to Deansgate and surrounding streets (which eventually came about in 1985). The council established a senior officer group to promote developments and reinvigorated the idea of a major project north of the Market Hall in particular.

Despite some other investments going ahead, little progress had been made with the provision of a recreation centre on the south side of the town centre as envisaged in 1965. In 1983 the council proposed the creation of a major project on land south of Great Moor Street, previously occupied by the railway, and which was largely in use as a car park. This mixed-use development was envisaged as a counterweight to the major retail proposals planned north of the Market Hall. The leisure and entertainment idea did not materialise in full, although it led to the construction of the Water Place leisure pool, designed by Faulkner-Brown, Hendy, Watkinson and Stonor, and formally opened by the Queen in 1988. Unfortunately, it subsequently closed in 2002, hampered by high maintenance costs and falling attendances.

Following a delay of several years caused by a poor investment climate, the council initiated a selection process for a developer of the major retail project north of the Market Hall and Grosvenor Developments were chosen. They began the construction of what was to become the Market Place in the autumn of 1985. The scheme, which was supported

Inside the Water Place in 1989.

Demolition of the Water Place in 2003.

Construction of the Market Place around 1986.

by a major urban development grant, included the refurbishment of the Market Hall to provide more than a quarter of a million square feet of retail space with Debenhams as the anchor store. Over 700 car parking spaces were also made available. The development was the most important element in a period which saw rising confidence and investment in the town centre generally.

In the 1990s the council launched a public-private Town Centre Partnership which issued a new Town Centre Strategy in 1997, aiming to ensure Bolton maintained its position as an important centre in the North West. It brought proposals together to improve transport arrangements, stimulate the arts and tourism, generate jobs and investment and to ensure public safety. Seven distinctive areas were identified in the town centre, each with a different emphasis – for example evening leisure, science and technology and an urban village. An area including the car park at the former Bullfield Sidings on Dean Road was identified as an important peripheral site which was subsequently developed for the colleges and university.

In 2002 the urban designers, Taylor Young, produced a plan for the area behind Victoria Hall, extending from Deansgate to St George's Road, known as Central Street, and covering 7.5 acres. Once again, a landmark development was proposed entailing a mixture of retail, leisure, commercial and residential uses. This attracted a development partner and was progressing well before it was cancelled in the wake of the financial crisis of 2007–08. Bolton was entering a challenging period of declining investor confidence.

A Town Centre Action Framework was published by the Bolton Vision Partnership in 2005. This considered the development of the town centre alongside the borough-wide strategies for economic development, transport, culture, and tourism, among others. It confirmed the need for a new transport interchange which was now to be located north of the station to bring bus and train services together, as well as an anti-clockwise gyratory system for bus services around the town centre. Key development areas were identified at Central Street, Church Wharf near the parish church, the railway station (for the interchange) and a cultural quarter to the west of Le Mans Crescent. Much of the private sector investment required failed to materialise, however.

In 2017 the Town Centre Strategy was refreshed, with 'intervention areas' established encircling most of the town centre. There was also a clear intention to tackle the area focussed on Crompton Place. A greater emphasis was being given to residential development. A £100 million fund was identified to see the strategy through and unlock private investment. By this time Bolton town centre was facing the challenges experienced by many established industrial towns including competition from internet sales, out-of-centre retail parks and the larger regional shopping centres. The future could perhaps involve a greater mixture of education, business, culture, leisure and residential uses, including student accommodation.

The modern Bolton transport interchange.

Most recently, plans have been unveiled to transform the former Magistrates' Court into a luxury hotel and a major revamp of Crompton Place and Victoria Square is in an advanced stage of planning, promoted by a partnership between the Beijing Construction Engineering Group and the Midia Group. Meanwhile, at the time of writing, the coronavirus pandemic has taken hold and the consequences for the future shape of the town (and the world in general) are uncertain. We wait to see what will transpire for the future of Bolton.

## DID YOU KNOW?

Peter Crook Marsden was the chairman of the council's Streets Committee which oversaw the construction of Marsden Road and its bridge. During its construction, the arch over the River Croal suffered a collapse, but the work was finally completed in 1877. Peter Marsden must have been pleased with the result because it was subsequently named after him. If this was during his lifetime it followed a practice which is not the policy today.

## DID YOU KNOW?

Some ad-hoc schemes were proposed in the town centre in the late 1950s/early 1960s. These included one by R. Seifert and Partners for land south of Great Moor Street, incorporating a new bus station, shopping, hotel, new railway station and new council offices. Another by Bernard Sunley Investment Trust proposed a large shopping scheme either side of Knowsley Street incorporating new premises for the Victoria Hall. Neither scheme succeeded.